MAKERS & SHAKERS

A HIDDEN HISTORY OF BLACK AMERICANS IN BOOZE

TROY HUGHES

Published by The History Press
An imprint of Arcadia Publishing
Charleston, SC
www.historypress.com

First published 2025

Manufactured in the United States

ISBN 9781467159517
Hardcover ISBN 9781540299901

Library of Congress Control Number: 2025939506

MAKERS & SHAKERS

This book is dedicated to my son, Isaac, and my daughter, Josephine. I keep telling you two that history is cool, and I hope that these stories about Black folks in and around booze along with some of the art, music and literature it has inspired helps you to realize this. The historical context for some of the stories is sometimes ugly, and I made it a point not to avoid or sugarcoat anything about how poorly we've been treated and thought of by our fellow Americans. Read with courage. I'll leave you with an apt quote that's been attributed to Golda Meir: "One cannot and must not try to erase the past merely because it does not fit the present."

I woke up this mornin' snake crawlin' in my hand

I woke up this mornin' snake crawlin' in my hand

He was crawlin' out that whiskey bottle, talking just like a natural man

Ah whiskey, oh whiskey, why do you treat me so?

—Josh White, "Pigmeat and Whiskey Blues," 1935

CONTENTS

Foreword, by Samara B. Davis 11
Preface 15
Playlist 19

1. Wine: A Tale of Two Virginians and the Unholy Trinity 21

2. Beer: Ted Mack Sr. and the Pretenders 31

3. "Brother Bootsie": The Cartoons of Ollie Harrington 38

4. Bertie "Birdie" Brown: Badass Montana Moonshiner 41

5. Colored Men Behind the Bar: A Brief Look at
   Some Early Bartenders 44

6. Milking and Murder in St. Louis:
   Meet Jack's Nephew Lem Motlow 52

7. Captain Clarence Webster: Hero and Booze Smuggler 62

8. Black Temperance: Bedimmed and Bedizzied 67

9. In the Clear: Tequila, Vodka and Gin 82

10. Distilled Spirits: Two Men of Firsts from the Big Apple 98

11. The White View on Blacks and the "Liquor Problem" from the Late 1890s 101
12. Cognac: Bloodthirsty Black Men and the Unofficial Spirit of Black America 110
13. Nigger Whiskey and Reconstruction 125
14. The Black Bourbon Society 133
15. Langston Hughes's Jesse B. Semple on the Drink 136
16. A Quick Trip Up North: Canadian Whisky 140
17. The Colonial Period: Rum and the Slave Trade 142
18. Malt Liquor: An Odyssey of Advertisement in Sight and Sound 151
19. Colonel Elmer Lucille Allen: Pioneering Woman Chemist 157

Bibliography 161
Index 173
About the Author 176

FOREWORD

When I first came into the spirits industry, eight and a half years ago, I came to it with one mission in mind: to prove that African Americans were an essential demographic to the success of the whiskey industry and should be recognized for their unwavering support over the years. Back then, my measure was a simple statistic: African Americans spent over $8.3 billion a year on wine, spirits and tobacco. That one statistic alone was enough for me to start gaining traction with brands that wanted to find out who these Black consumers were through my newly founded social group, Black Bourbon Society.

I grew up a total '80s kid. I remember Billy Dee Williams posing with Colt 45 in centerfold advertisements in *Ebony* and *Jet* magazine. I remember the commercials showcasing "black elegance" featuring Seagram's Gin. Those products embedded themselves in my brain early as something that Black folks with money and class incorporated into their sophisticated lives—what we now know to be cheap malt liquor and bottom-of-the-barrel gin.

In my teenage years, I saw how hip-hop became the way spirits brands reached younger demographics. Wu-Tang promoted St. Ides, Biggie Smalls rapped about Cristal champagne and I will forever have that St. Ides jingle sung by Snoop and Nate Dogg stuck in my head. Busta Rhymes' "Pass the Courvoisier" became the theme song for my college years. T-Pain crooned "Buy U a Drank," and every club night ended with Jamie Foxx telling us to "blame it on the a-a-a-a-a-alcohol."

And as I got older, much older, I remember driving through South Central Los Angeles with my mother and noticing that on every corner there was either a liquor store, a gas station or a church. As we drove deeper into the hood, we'd sometimes see all three on the same block! Posters advertising alcohol covered abandoned buildings like wallpaper. It was everywhere. Add that to the urban landscape of people walking up and down these streets begging for money to "buy a beer" or get a pack of cigarettes, and I realized that the reality of drinking malt liquor was nothing like the glamourous magazine ads I saw as a kid. Instead, I literally saw it destroying my community.

One might think that after all I observed, I would have started a crusade to protest the predatory marketing strategies the spirits industry used on the Black community. But instead, I saw an opportunity to prove that there was a responsible way to engage Black consumers built on education and appreciation. And over the years, we've done just that.

But in proving this very compelling point to brands, there was one thing my perspective lacked: historical knowledge. A year after I launched Black Bourbon Society, the story of Nathan Nearest Green, the first African American master distiller on record, surfaced in great detail, and a brand was named after him to cement his legacy in the spirits industry forever. This confirmed what many in the spirits industry have always suspected: that Black Americans have played a vital role in the production of whiskey and other spirits in this country since colonial slavery. We knew, however, that like other history, our stories and contributions were conveniently lost and forgotten—and that some of the largest brands today would never have survived without these contributions, especially those that were the result of free labor.

This is what makes Troy's research in this book so valuable. Like Troy's first book, which uncovered the richly diverse community of Mount Pleasant in Washington, D.C., *Makers & Shakers: A Hidden History of Black Americans in Booze* sheds light on a myriad of Black contributors across historical and modern timelines, this time in the world of spirits. All these accounts—some personal testimonies from the past, others stories (sometimes tragic and mysterious) buried in newspaper clippings—were never meant to be rediscovered and collated into a body of work that connects them to a larger purpose. This is a history that spirits enthusiasts, like BBS members and industry professionals, like my colleagues and I, can now reference and glean wisdom from.

There are many rabbit holes to get lost in while reading this book. One story that caught my eye was that of Miss Bertie Brown, a young Black woman making "hooch" during Prohibition in Montana, of all places. Her story is not just one of a moonshine contributor but one of a woman who defied many odds, considering the historical context and the political landscape at that time. She was a well-respected, educated Black woman who owned her own property in the early 1930s—in Montana. By all accounts, she was making damn good moonshine and stayed busy selling her product throughout Prohibition. A mystery surrounds her death, though. Was it an accident? Or was it a fated result of the typical discrimination and terrorization that successful African Americans and African American communities experienced during that time? I don't know if I'll ever let this story go until Troy can dig up more information on it; it is absolutely fascinating.

This is why this book is so important. We've been intentionally disassociated from Black stories in the spirits industry so that we stay at the bottom of the industry's ecosystem—as consumers being fed false advertising and hip-hop jingles that stay stuck our heads for over thirty years. If the story of Bertie Brown was readily known, can you imagine how many Black female distillers would have been bold enough to follow in her footsteps? It would take another eighty-seven years before a Black woman in my industry would even consider going into the field of distilling spirits. My colleagues and I thought we were the first to break barriers in this industry. To be honest, we're glad that we are not.

We, like Troy, are called to reclaim and retell our history while successfully contributing and making our own history in this industry. Combine my life's work to prove the value of the Black consumer in this industry with what Troy is doing through this book in proving our existence in this industry, and you've got enough energy to start a Black bourbon revolution. Now, I don't know if I want to lead that, but as per usual, I'm sure Troy will document the growth and success of that in his next book, too.

They say the truth always finds a way to the light. God bless the storytellers who capture it for all of us to see.

Cheers!

—Samara B. Davis

PREFACE

Black history and culture have been intertwined with the manufacture, sale and use of alcoholic beverages in the United States since the beginning. This book pulls together selected historical and contemporary stories about alcohol, in all its varied varieties, to show how it has played a part in the fascinating and often ugly history of Black people in the United States. (Trigger warning: The N-word appears a lot in this book!)

The idea for this book was born in Louisville, Kentucky, in September 2023. I was there to attend the annual convention of the Black Bourbon Society (BBS), called the Bourbon Boule. I was a part of the BBS's program called BOSS, which stands for Black Owned Spirits Symposium. Yep, I'm the co-owner of a liquor company: Mt. P. Craft Spirits in Washington, D.C. BOSS was a cohort of selected small spirit brand owners who were given the opportunity to meet and interact with industry leaders in an attempt to kickstart their respective brands.

In Louisville, the BOSS Babies, as we were called, were given the opportunity to share samples of our products with convention attendees in a room called the Sip Suite. (A quick shout-out to my fellow BOSS Baby brands: Casa Reyes Tequila, Greenwood Whiskey, Redd Rose Vodka and Red Hazel Whiskey.) While I was dutifully pouring samples of our Mt. Pleasant Club Whiskey and telling BBS members about my first book, *Whiskey Makers in Washington, D.C.: A Pre-Prohibition History*, recounting the stories of the all-White whiskey guys that inhabit those pages—I knew that I wanted to find and tell the stories of Black folk and alcohol. I figured that

BOOTSIE By OLLIE HARRINGTON

"Yaas, Brother Bootsie, I know 'bout them scientists, too, who writes books 'bout how you're supposed to see visual apparitions if you drinks good whiskey, but, Brother, you reckon we has had THAT MUCH good whiskey?"

Bootsie, by Ollie Harrington, April 11, 1959. *From the* Pittsburgh Courier *Archives*.

there had to be way more stories than just Uncle Nearest's that were worth telling, and boy was I right.

As with any endeavor such as this, there are numerous folks who were instrumental in getting this book published. First, I must thank my acquisitions editor, John Rodrigue, who shepherded this manuscript through the process and got it approved for publication—I know how much of a stretch this book is for The History Press. Many thanks to my guy in Pennsylvania, the whiskey maker and liquor merchant Aaron Kendeall. He brought Captain Clarence Webster to my attention. Be on the lookout for some sort of liquor honoring the good captain sometime in the future. Next up is Christina Owens Knapp (https://hellowyellow.com), who provided the most excellent drawings of J. June Lewis's wine bottles. A giant thanks goes out to my image guy, the jack of all trades, Jason Hamacher (https://lostorigins.gallery). All the photos and scans (including the upsampled images that had to be restored before they could be used) included in the book are due to him—except for the author photo, which was taken by my son, Isaac F.B. Hughes. A heartfelt thanks to Samara Davis for writing the foreword and for opening up my whiskey world by including me as one of her BOSS Babies. And last but not least, thanks to my business partner and Whiskey Brother, John Loughner. We are still having fun!

April 2025

WHAT DO I CALL MY PEOPLE?

As you'll see, throughout history, Black people have been called all sort of names. In this book, when I have a choice, I refer to those of the Negroid persuasion as simply Black—even though all of us (including "white people") are actually a shade of brown. Correspondingly, I refer to our Caucasoid brothers and sisters as White—even though, as my daughter points out, they are more sort of peach in color to her eye.

In performing the research for and writing this book, I relied on lots and lots of newspaper articles, advertisements, obituaries, images and song lyrics, along with scholarly articles and blog posts. Any omissions or inaccuracies are my sole responsibility.

I want to give a special shout-out to Allen Cannon, a man who has worn many hats since I met him almost twenty years ago: a former colleague at the law firm Perkins Coie (yes, one of the firms that is the subject of one of those BS executive orders), a friend, a mentor and even the godfather to one of my kids. Allen, thanks for taking the time to carefully read the manuscript that became this book. I'm quite pleased that it did indeed "piss you off."

PLAYLIST

As you read this book, keep this playlist of songs in mind, as it will help capture the spirit of the stories being told. Find the Makers & Shakers: The Hidden History of Black Americans in Booze playlist by searching for "the masked nostalgia" profile on Spotify.

1. "Blame It" (2008), Jamie Foxx
2. "(What's the Word) Thunderbird" (1958), The Casual-Aires
3. "Tequila" (1958), The Champs
4. "Peppermint Twist" (1961), Joey Dee and the Starliters
5. "Night Train" (1961), James Brown
6. "Let Us Help the Colored People" (1880), National WCTU Publishing House
7. "Nightrain" (1987), Guns N' Roses
8. "Lightnin' Bar Blues" (1973), Brownsville Station
9. "Beers and Sunshine" (2020), Darius Rucker
10. "One Mint Julep" (1952), the Clovers
11. "Ciroc & Simply Lemonade" (2013), Nelly
12. "Devil's Island Gin Blues" (1934), Roosevelt "Honeydripper" Sykes
13. "Gin and Juice" (1993), Snoop Dogg
14. "Patrol of the Picaninnies" (1915), I.J. Masten

15. "Hennessy" (2004), Tupac Shakur
16. "Pass the Courvoisier" (2002), Busta Rhymes featuring Diddy and Pharrell Williams
17. "The Dancing Deacon" (1918), Hell Fighters Band, 369th U.S. Infantry Band and James Reece Europe
18. "On Patrol in No Man's Land" (1918), Hell Fighters Band, 369th U.S. Infantry Band and James Reece Europe
19. "The Humpty Dance" (1990), Digital Underground
20. "Essence of Old Virginny/Sebastopol Breakdown" (2007), Tim Twiss
21. "A Bar Song (Tipsy)" (2024), Shaboozey
22. "Blues and Booze" (1924), Ma Rainey
23. "Shots" (2009), LMFAO featuring Lil Jon
24. "Drinking Blues" (1934), Lucille Bogan
25. "Bad Liquor Blues" (1935), Scrapper Blackwell
26. "Booze Crazy Man Blues" (1928), Ida Cox
27. "Pigmeat and Whiskey Blues" (1935), Joshua White
28. "Bad Whiskey Blues" (1947), Merline Johnson
29. "Drunk Again" (1954), Champion Jack Dupree
30. "Molasses to Rum" (1969), Sherman Edwards
31. "Whiskey, Women and Loaded Dice" (1954), Joe Liggins
32. "I Wasn't Thinking, I Was Drinking" (1954), The Checkers
33. "Hey Bartender" (1955), Floyd Dixon
34. "Drinkin Wine Spo-Dee-O-Dee" (1949), Wynonie Harris
35. "One Bourbon, One Scotch, One Beer" (1974), John Lee Hooker
36. "Cheers (Drink to That)" (2010), Rihanna
37. "Sloppy Drunk" (1972), Jimmy Rodgers
38. "One Scotch, One Bourbon, One Beer" (1953), Amos Milburn and His Aladdin Chickenshackers
39. "Fine Booze and Heavy Dues" (1962), Lonnie Johnson
40. "Pour Out a Little Liquor" (1994), Thug Life
41. "8 Ball" (1987), N.W.A.
42. "1 Million Bottlebags" (1991), Public Enemy

CHAPTER 1

WINE

A TALE OF TWO VIRGINIANS AND THE UNHOLY TRINITY

If you wanna get along in some strange town
Buy some wine an' pass it around
All them cats will think you fine
All of them cats, they love sweet wine
—*"Drinkin' Wine Spo-Dee-O-Dee," Wynonie Harris, 1949*

There are two interesting stories that I wanted to tell here, both of men from Virginia: one made wine for years and one—not so much. After that, we visit the strange world of the fortified and carbonated wines and look at three creations from the Gallo brothers.

RAYMOND FEDDERMAN AND THE "WINERY" THAT NEVER HAD A CHANCE

The November 16, 1973 *New York Times* article titled "For the 'First Black Winery in the U.S.,' 1973 Was NOT a Good Year" prepares us for a tale of woe. The article explains how in 1944, Ray Fedderman made his first trip north to Prattsburgh, New York (thirty miles northwest of Elmira), from his home in Virginia, where he was previously a sharecropper. He had come to help pick potatoes. Ray recounted how, after the truck he was traveling in broke down in Harrisburg, Pennsylvania, he had to spend all but his last five cents to get the truck back on the road. Ray continued:

When we got here [Prattsburgh] *I went into a restaurant for a cup of coffee. I was 29 years old and I'd never been in a restaurant with whites before. When a white woman sat next to me I rattled that damn cup and spilled my five cents worth of coffee on the counter.*

Rosalind White label, Fedderman Wine Co. Inc. *Jason Hamacher.*

Eventually, Ray got over his nervousness, and because the potato growers in New York weren't as efficient as those back in Virginia, Ray was able to introduce practices up there that earned him some renown in local farming circles. He did so well that in 1954, when the farming company he'd been working for wanted to sell its New York operation, Ray was able to acquire most of the property (about six hundred acres). Over time, Ray added to his holdings: he had a janitorial service, a car wash, a grocery store and a coin laundry. Ray was a player. With his empire in this rural corner of the world flourishing, circa 1970, Ray was given the idea to open a winery by one Walter S. Taylor, who went on to make a splash in the New York State wine scene.

AN ASIDE: DAVID VERSUS GOLIATH IN THE FINGER LAKES

In the early 1970s, Walter S. Taylor was the scion of the Taylor Wine Company, which had been making wine in the area since the 1880s. Walter was exiled from the company in 1970, when he made the mistake of speaking loudly against local winemaking practices, particularly attacking the use of California grapes in New York wines. He did this in front of wine executives gathered in San Francisco, and apparently the Taylor Wine Company board (which included many members of his family) wasn't too cool with what he said, so they gave him the choice of resigning or being fired. He chose the latter and opened up his own winery at Bully Hill, which was the original home of Taylor Wine. In time, because Walter was such a showman, Bully Hill Wines, with names like Meat Market Red and Old Trawler White, became the best known wine brand in New York State.

When Coca-Cola acquired the Taylor Wine Company in 1977, it quickly went after Walter, getting a court order barring him from promoting any link to the Taylor name and forbidding his use of that name in any form. Walter, being Walter, fought back by creating labels for his wines such as one with a goat on it and the slogan, "They have my name, and my heritage, but they didn't get my goat." Another label featured an owl saying, "Walter S. Who?"

It was around this time (the late '60s) that Walter, who had known Ray for years, planted the idea for Ray to get into the wine business. At the same time, Walter was setting up his Bully Hill Winery. Ray got to work trying to raise money for his own winery. He decided to try to get a Small Business Administration (SBA) loan to the tune of $350,000. Because of his business empire, he thought the application process was a mere formality. In the year leading up to the opening of his winery, Ray spent a lot of his time working at Walter's winery, learning the trade. The plan was for Ray to first buy wine in bulk and just bottle it to start.

April 1972 brought the start of construction on Ray's winery, and June that year brought some devastating floods to the area. Though Prattsburgh was spared, Ray later claimed that the SBA lost interest in finalizing his loan, preferring to focus on helping other small businesses in the area recover from the floods. At any rate, his money was running out as the expected new SBA loan did not materialize. When the Fedderman Winery opened for business on June 1, 1972, there were two wines to choose from: the Irene Red, named after Ray's wife, and the Rosalind White, named after his business partner Charles Young's wife. The *New York Times* article concluded that with his financing up in the air,

> *distributors began to refuse to take any more of his wine because they thought he would not be in business much longer. But one distributor, who asked not to be named, said he simply could not interest any of his customers in the Fedderman wines.*
>
> *Mr. Fedderman agrees now that his operation was not overly efficient at the outset and that his outright appeal to black consumers may not have been good marketing. But he has a new bottle design and a new label that talks about the product rather than the fact that it is made in "The First Black Winery in the United States."*

One month after the *New York Times* article was published, in December 1973, another article appeared in a local newspaper that continued the chronicle of Fedderman's winery, titled "Money Woes, but No Sour Grapes for Winemaker." The author noted that the winery was "an operation that will surely go down in the books of black history" and that Fedderman remained confident the SBA money would materialize. He was quoted as saying: "It's been rough, brother, I can tell you that....But its going to get better. You gotta roll with the punches, that's all." In describing Fedderman's operation, the article indicated that the "winery" was a 100-by-55-foot metal building that contained the bottling equipment. The wine Fedderman used came from a winery in nearby Batavia, where the grapes were pressed to his specifications. He commented that "there was no way he could get into the whole winemaking thing."

Fedderman recounted how the winery received over one hundred phone calls from people wanting to order his wine after the *New York Times* piece appeared, but because it was illegal to ship wines via the mail or other carriers, it only "helped psychologically, the calls didn't do much financially." Ever the optimist, Fedderman concluded, "We are going to have a watermelon and peach wine coming out that we think will be big. We're working on another wine, kind of unusual but when we get the permits, it should be something else."

Unfortunately, that "unusual" wine never made it to fruition, and the next time Fedderman appeared in the news was when he attended the auction of the equipment and other assets of his previous winery. In a July 3, 1974 article, Fedderman was quoted as saying, "They put me out of business. They put me out of business because I am black. I thought we had overcome the deal of picking on a person 'cause of the color of his skin." It only took the auctioneer eighty minutes to dispose of the assets. The 4,740 remaining bottles of Rosalind White Wine were sold for ten cents a bottle.

It's obvious that Fedderman didn't have a subscription to the *Durham Morning Herald*, because if he had, he would have learned about his fellow Black Virginian, John June Lewis, from the July 30, 1972 edition of the newspaper. It turns out that Lewis, who went by June, had been running his own winery since 1940.

J. June Lewis: A Labor of Love

To properly tell June's story, we need to start with his father, Armistead Burwell (1840–1920). The Burwells were among the first families in the Colony of Virginia. Armistead's one-thousand-acre property was called

Woburn Plantation. During the Civil War, he enlisted in Company E of the Fourteenth Virginia Regiment, called the Clarksville Blues. He served periodically, as he was often ill or injured. One such injury was sustained on May 16, 1864, at the Battle of Drewry's Bluff: a gunshot wound to the left thigh. After recovering, he served as a nurse at General Hospital No. 1 in Kittrell Springs, North Carolina. As documented in his last will and testament, his desire was "to be buried in the family burying ground, and soon thereafter as may be convenient, my executors shall cause to be erected over my grave a neat marble tombstone with such inscription as they think proper and underneath said inscription the words, 'A Confederate Soldier.'"

In the 1890 and 1900 U.S. Censuses, June's mother, Anna Lewis, was listed as a Black female "farmer." Her son John (June) was listed as Black as well. In the 1910 census, June was listed as "mulatto servant with the occupation of farm laborer, living in the household of Confederate Veteran, Armistead Burwell, aged 70." At the age of seventy-eight, during an interview that was incorporated into the 1972 newspaper article, June recalled asking Armistead about the Civil War:

> *I'd ask him questions about the war, and he'd say, "Lord, Lord, don't ask em 'bout that infernal war." You know I sorta thought that word "infernal" was a curse word, but I looked it up in the dictionary. You know it means having to do with the devil.*
>
> *Burwell was wounded twice in the Civil War. I said I never would'a come back the second time, and he said, "I was fightin' for my country."*

June also fought for his country, albeit a different one—the United States, as opposed to the Confederate States. After World War I, in 1919, he served as part of the American Army of Occupation. His draft card states that he was employed by "A. Burwell in the occupation of farming and manufacturing lumber contract." While in the U.S. Army, June served in the Rhine Valley in Europe, and it was there that he gained a "heightened appreciation for viticulture and viniculture." There are stories that Armistead Burwell may have taught him how to grow grapes growing up. After his return, June was listed in the 1920 census as a "hired man" associated with the occupation of "saw mill" in the household of A. Burwell, age seventy-nine. Eventually, Burwell deeded June the family farm.

Right after the repeal of Prohibition in 1933, June began growing grapes on an eight- to ten-acre patch of his property. He opened his Woburn Winery in 1940. He must have needed a few grapes to round out what he grew for bottling the first batch. In the September 19, 1940 edition of the *Henderson Daily Dispatch*, we find this:

> *WANT TO BUY GRAPES IN large quantities.*
> *J. June Lewis. Woburn Winery, Clarksville, VA., route 1*

June's wine was called Virginia–Carolina Brand, an apt name given that his property is indeed on the Virginia-North Carolina border. His winery was listed in pretty much every edition of the *Wines & Vines Annual Directory*. As for his clientele, the 1972 article quotes one of his sons:

> *We've been here 32 years. Most of our customers come back year after year, and some buy a bottle and some a case. There is no thought about going big time or commercial, he adds: "The only way to do that is to go to concentrate or that old fortified stuff.... We have some tobacco and cattle and the wine business. We're making a good living. It's a labor of love, really.*

In order to get his Virginia Alcoholic Beverage Control (ABC) license, June had to incorporate his business. He commented in the article, "That Virgina ABC Board, they been mighty good to me." In the September 15, 1949 *Richmond Times-Dispatch*, we find this notice regarding his ABC license:

> *THIS is to notify the public that on Sept. 25, 1949, I will apply to the Virginia Alcoholic Beverage Control Board for wholesale license to sell wine at Woburn Winery, B-W-16, Clarksville, VA., Route 1.*
> *Said wine to be consumed off said premises.*
> *J. June Lewis*

A similar notice can be found in the May 5, 1958 edition of the same newspaper.

Running the winery was a family affair, for the most part. June was president, a close family friend named

Top: Virginia-Carolina Brand Raisin Wine; *bottom*: Virginia-Carolina Brand Virginia Red Grape Wine. *Christina Owens Knapp*.

Sign above the front door of Woburn Winery No. 16. *Christina Owens Knapp.*

William H. Reid was vice president, the treasurer was John June Lewis Jr. (also known as "Duckie") and the secretary was another son named, I kid you not, Schwarzkopf Lewis, a 1954 graduate of Howard University. June died in 1974, and the winery closed soon thereafter.

FORTIFIED AND CARBONATED WINES: THE UNHOLY TRINITY (THUNDERBIRD, NIGHT TRAIN AND RIPPLE)

In 1954, a change to the federal regulations concerning wine was enacted, and it led to a revolution. That change was the addition of "Subpart S—Special Natural Wine" to 26 Code of Federal Regulations (CFR) Section 240, in part section 240.440.

> Materials. *Special Natural Wine is a flavored wine made on bonded wine cellar premises from a base of natural wine. The flavoring added may include herbs, spices, fruit juices, natural aromatics, natural essences, or other natural flavorings, in such quantities or proportions that the resulting products derives a distinctive flavor from their use, and may be distinguished from natural wine not so treated.*

Boy, were some distinctive flavors achieved. With that addition to the CFR, "bum wine" (cheap fortified wines with an ABV between 13 and 20 percent) were officially recognized by the government. First out of the gate with a 1954 release was Richards Wild Irish Rose.

WHAT'S THE WORD? THUNDERBIRD!

The Gallo brothers, Ernest and Julio, were next. In the early 1950s, acting on a tip from one of their sales managers, who'd observed that certain customers at local inner-city liquor stores would buy port wine and add lemon juice or lemon Kool-Aid mix to it, the Gallos got to work to make a lemon-flavored wine that would suit those inner-city customers. After much trial and error in the lab, they arrived at formulation for Thunderbird. The name was coined by one Albion Fenderson, a Gallo sales manager who just happened to be an amateur scholar of Native American folklore. It probably didn't hurt that Ford had just introduced a brand-new sports car with the same name in 1955. The marketing campaign designed for the roll-out was big. They hired the Cisco Kid, Cesar Romero (who later went on to be the first Joker in *Batman*), for the TV spots and ran this 1957 jingle on radio stations across the country:

What's the word? Thunderbird!
How's it sold? Good and cold.
What's the jive? Bird's alive.
What's the price? Thirty twice.

They also hired a "Princess Thunderbird," a woman dressed in a revealing Native American outfit who had the job of charming retailers at live promotions and giving out free samples. In 1958, the musical group the Casual-Aires released a song called "(What's the Word) Thunderbird"—which sounds a lot like the Champs' "Tequila," which came out the same year. Regarding the price, "thirty twice" was sixty cents—a truly affordable wine. I recall hearing the jingle growing up in the 1970s, but the price was "twice nice"—two dollars, I guess. Another great

"(What's the Word) Thunderbird" by the Casual-Aires. *Jason Hamacher.*

TV ad from 1977 gave us the new "Shake 'Em Up" to a disco tune. A Black couple grooved on the dance floor while telling us to mix Thunderbird with grapefruit juice and "shake 'em up"—yum. The rollout was a huge success, and the wine acquired the street names Chicken and Pluck. It was reported that illiterate customers would peel the label off the bottle to show liquor store clerks what it was they wanted. In one famous account, often retold, multimillionaire Ernest Gallo was in Atlanta when he saw a gentleman with a bottle of Thunderbird on the street and exclaimed, "What's the word?" To which he received the reply, "Thunderbird!"

ALL ABOARD: THE NIGHT TRAIN EXPRESS

After the success of Thunderbird, the Gallo boys sought to concoct the next big flavored wine. Along the way, they had a few flops. There was Cherokee, which was marketed to a Native American audience. The chieftain on the label wore a Sioux headdress, and when salesmen put Cherokee in front of members of the Hopi and Navajo Nations, it did not go well. Twister was the name of a peppermint-flavored wine that sought to capitalize on the dance craze that started at New York City's Peppermint Lounge (128 West Forty-Fifth Street). Check out Joey Dee and the Starliters' 1961 song "Peppermint Twist" for a shoutout to Forty-Fifth Street. Gypsy Rose was a shameless attempt to counter the competition in the form of Richards Wild Irish Rose. And finally, there was the ill-timed "oriental wine" that Gallo named Hai Tori, which came out as the Vietnam War raged. It didn't last long.

Night Train Express was introduced in the early 1960s and proved to be that next big hit for Gallo. It had the street name Ticket. In a dismissive review, one wine critic noted that it was a "ticket to nowhere," which is sort of the point when you're drinking bum wine, right? There is speculation that the name was inspired by either James Brown's 1961 hit "Night Train" or one of the National Football League's first Black superstars, Dick "Night Train" Lane, who played for the Los Angeles Rams from 1952 to '53, the Chicago Cardinals from 1954 to '59 and Detroit Lions from 1960 to '65. With their 1987 song, "Nightrain," Guns N'Roses paid tribute to the band's early days, highlighting the wine's importance to their daily calorie intake: "I'm on the nightrain, love the stuff. I'm on the nightrain, I can never get enough." The train ran for a long time, but Gallo pulled it off the shelf for good with no fanfare in 2016.

RIPPLE: THE NATIONAL DRINK OF WATTS

The same 1954 regulation change that birthed fortified wines also birthed its milder cousin, carbonated wine:

> *If effervescent special natural wine is to be produced, either naturally or by artificial carbonation, the requirements of subpart W of this part…must be followed.*

Indeed, Gallo must have met the requirements of subpart W, because in 1960, they introduced Ripple, which was marketed to the casual drinker, as its ABV reached only 11 percent. Boone's Farm, another Gallo product, was birthed in 1961. In the early 1970s, Ripple got some great product placement on the sitcom *Sanford and Son*, which aired from 1972 to '78. Redd Foxx's Fred G. Sandford almost single-handedly made the drink popular. Ripple was mentioned often on the sitcom as Fred's drink of choice and the "National Drink of Watts." Here are a few of the drinks Fred concocted:

Flipple:	*Sangria and Ripple*
Champiple:	*Champagne and Ripple or ginger ale and Ripple*
Manischipple:	*Manischewitz and Ripple*
Beaujolipple:	*Beaujolais and Ripple*
Cripple:	*Cream and Ripple*
Stipple:	*Straight Ripple*
Flapple:	*Flat Ripple or Sangria*
Muscatipple:	*Muscatel and Ripple*
Mintchipple:	*Mint julep and Ripple*

Ripple came in three flavors: Original, Pear and Pagan Pink. A short-lived spinoff of Pagan Pink, called "Tickled Pink," featured radio ads where an announcer spoke in a very exaggerated Black dialect that was considered offensive. Check out Brownsville Station's 1973 "Lighting Bar Blues" for a mention of the carbonated wine. Ripple was pulled off the shelves in 1984, a victim of the wine cooler fad.

CHAPTER 2

BEER

TED MACK SR. AND THE PRETENDERS

I want to get away from this blackness and whiteness—I didn't buy this brewery for black power.…There is only one kind of power in this country and that's green power—money.
—Theodore Mack Sr.

Yeah, the only BS I need is beers and sunshine.
—Darius Rucker, 2020

BLIND JOHN RANDOLPH AND HIS "OLD COLONY BREWERY"

The first press regarding Black ownership of a brewery in the United States came in the form of a slew of articles appearing in Black newspapers (the *Alabama Tribune*, the *Black Dispatch*, the *New York Age*, the *Pittsburgh Courier* and the *Jackson Advocate*) starting in early December 1955. The article from the *Jackson Advocate* read:

FIRST NEGRO-OWNED BREWERY
LAUNCHED IN PHILADELPHIA

PHILADELPHIA, Pa., Nov. 28—A pioneering move in American business was launched here last week at a huge banquet when the first Negro in the history of beer brewing unveiled his product before an audience of civic leaders, distributors, and tavern owners.

Open Brewery—Blind John Randolph Smith, shown with his wife, Verna, launched the Colony House Brewing Company in Trenton, N. J., making his product the first beer on sale on the American market owned and operated by a Negro company.

"Open Brewery—Blind John Randolph Smith," December 3, 1955. *From the* Pittsburgh Courier *Archives.*

> *Making his entry into the multimillion-dollar industry, John Randolph Smith makes history. Mr. Smith, formerly of Atlanta, Ga., lost his sight at the early age of seven. This misfortune did not retard his progress but served as an incentive to his business career.*
>
> *Entering the highly competitive brewery field with a premium beer under the label, "Colony House," Mr. Smith announced that 50 metropolitan cities had already been selected as prospectible distribution areas.*
>
> *This will afford an opportunity for Negroes to invest in the wholesale beer distribution at a local level—along the Eastern seaboard, Midwest, and Southwest sections of the country. There is no instance, heretofore, on record wherein a Negro has attempted the brewery business at a brewery and bottling level.*

Sounds great, right? The thing is, after this initial barrage of articles, there was nary a mention of Colony House as a beer brand—despite the articles mentioning that Smith and his wife, Verna, had traveled "more than 7,000 miles consulting expert brewers and testing brews in perfecting this formula for Colony House." Simply crickets. There's been speculation that the article was written to stir up interest in wholesale distribution opportunities, but who knows?

SUNSHINE BREWING COMPANY

The next candidate for the first Black-owned brewery in the United States is the Sunshine Brewing Company, out of Reading, Pennsylvania. The year was 1969, and a group of Black entrepreneurs from Philadelphia, led by Walter Bantom and A. Bart Starr, was announced as the new owner of the brewery. Apparently, the group was founded by Leo Israel Bloom (the brewery's recently deposed owner) and was convened to secure a SBA loan for about half a million dollars through a local bank. In addition to the brewery, the group's money was used to form ARC Distributing in Richmond, Virginia—which was to be Sunshine's exclusive distributor. The brewery had a new product, called "Jamaica Sun Premium Beer" that it was trying to market to Blacks.

Bloom originally got a group of investors from Reading to bankroll his purchase of Sunshine in 1964. He became the president of the company and together with Anthony Sicilian, who ran an outfit called Cold Beer Distribution in New York City, began draining the company of money. After three years of mismanagement, selling beer for less than it cost to produce and giving away huge quantities as inducements to purchase more, the company went into receivership in 1967, and Bloom was forced out as president.

According to Sicilian, the new owners ran the brewery for about a year, and during that time, they "took every penny out of the company they could." In 1970, just before the brewery went out of business for a second time, *Brewers' Digest* ran a cover story proclaiming that Sunshine was having a record year and looking forward to a "Sunny" future. The article also highlighted that Sunshine and ARC Distributing were the only Black-owned companies in the industry.

In the February 4, 1971 edition of the *Evening Herald* newspaper from Shenandoah, Pennsylvania, an article titled "Sunshine Brewing Co., Up for Sale" reported:

> *According to an announcement made yesterday, the Sunshine Brewing Co., of Reading will be sold at a sheriff's sale on March 5.*
>
> *The brewery, in its 20th year of operation under the name of Sunshine, has faced change of ownership, expansion, and increased production. In the last 3 years it has become bogged down in debt and on several occasions appealed for court aid to save the business under the bankruptcy laws.*

There is no mention of the owners being Black, but the article does mention Bloom, the company's ex-president, saying that he had a federal tax lien notice for failure to pay withholding and Social Security taxes for 1967. In the end, Bloom was arrested, and he turned state's evidence in an organized crime trial in 1971. The brewery was seized by one of its creditors and sold off piece by piece. Nothing remained, and the Black investors just faded into the ether.

PEOPLES BREWERY, OSHKOSH, WISCONSIN

The story of Theodore "Ted" Mack Sr. and how he spearheaded the purchase of and ran the Peoples Brewing Company in Oshkosh, Wisconsin, is one that has been told before but is worth retelling here. Mack was born in Alabama in 1930, and despite having scholarship offers from a number of Black colleges, he opted to serve in the U.S. Army during the Korean War. After his discharge from the military, he was offered and accepted a football scholarship to Ohio State University. He soon transferred to Marquette University in Milwaukee, in 1955. Unfortunately, prior to playing any games for the Warriors, he suffered a career-ending injury. He graduated as the only Black student in his class with a degree in social work. Mack first went to work for the Milwaukee County Welfare Department and was drawn to social and economic activism to try to bring about positive change for the area's Black community. He chaired several civil rights organizations and even organized a bus to attend the 1963 March on Washington.

Mack eventually ended up with a job at Pabst Brewing Company: head of production and industrial relations. He was hired in part to help Pabst recruit more Black production workers, likely due to the passage of the Civil Rights Act of 1964, Title VII of which allowed minorities to file lawsuits against companies based on employment discrimination. Up until that time, breweries had an appalling paucity of Black workers. While at Pabst, Mack took the opportunity to learn as much about the different departments that made up the brewery as he could.

In 1969, the opportunity to acquire a brewery in the area presented itself. Pabst, facing antitrust concerns, was being forced to sell one of its affiliates, Blatz Brewery in Milwaukee. Mack put together a group of Black businessmen who established an entity called United Black Enterprises (UBE). The entity cobbled together a $9 million offer to purchase Blatz

Peoples Beer can. *Jason Hamacher.*

but ultimately was outbid by over $2 million by G. Heilman Brewing Company of La Crosse, Wisconsin. About the setback, Mack said, "We did it your way....I don't know what method we'll use next time, but we'll be back." UBE didn't have to wait long: within the year, they approached the Oshkosh-based Peoples Brewing Company with a $600,000 offer, which was accepted by the brewery's 135 shareholders in April 1970. Of the offer, $400,000 came from an SBA loan as part of President Nixon's "black capitalism" minority business plan.

Even before the bid was accepted, Mack faced adversity. On the day the offer was accepted (April 14), the *Milwaukee Sentinel* ran a story suggesting that if the sale went through, Mack would replace the brewery's White employees with Black ones from Milwaukee and change the brewery's name and beer. The story took off, and local Oshkosh taverns pulled Peoples from their taps in retaliation. James Mathers, who would go on to become mayor of Oshkosh, recalled that the morning the article came out, he overheard a resident say, "Well, we better beef up, the niggers are coming to town."

Mack held a press conference a few weeks later and addressed the issues head-on. The April 27, 1970 edition of the *Oshkosh Northwestern* documented his responses in an article titled "Falsehoods Rapped by Brewery President." Mack began by stating, "We're not making any black beer—if you see a beer you like, you should buy it." He was crystal clear on the goal of the press conference:

> *To try and stymie some of the falsehoods being circulated in both Oshkosh and Milwaukee about the operation of the brewery and other matters.*
>
> *We are not changing the name of the company, or the brand (of beer) and we will continue to employee all the personnel that's there. Our board of directors will be integrated and as we increase production, we will hire whoever wants to work for us.*
>
> *I'm not a black superman that can move people here and there. I'm coming here to produce beer—I'm not here to bring black people here or to bring white people here.*

When asked if it were true that the company had lost its brewmaster, Mack declared, "Not unless he's left in the last 15 minutes and as far as I know everyone else is staying." In response to a reporter who asked about the loss of sales since the company was put on the market, Mack said:

> *Myself and Oshkosh are very much on the spot. This is regarded as one of the most bigoted cities in the country, north and south. If sales are down, it will be a black eye on Oshkosh, not me. I can hold up on my end. It is a matter of whether Oshkosh can hold up its end.*

Indeed, in 1970, the Black population of Oshkosh was 103, while the White was 50,000. Mack attempted to bring players from the Green Bay Packers into the mix. He mentioned that many of the Black football players would be watching to see the city and the surrounding area's reaction to the change in ownership of the brewery. He noted that White players like Max McGee and Bart Starr could have big businesses in the area, but also remarked, "What did [the area] ever do for [the Black] Willie Davis, Herb Adderley or Wille Wood?"

Mack continued:

> *I didn't get this far by osmosis, but by hard work, by saving my capital, and by getting along with men. I grew up in Alabama…where they threw rocks at me and called me "nigger." …I don't scare easily.…I will not run, no sir. I believe in content of character, rather than in pigmentation of skin. I wish there could be love between my white brothers and I.…I'm coming here to stay although I've been told by many people, whites and blacks, that this is not the town to come to.*
>
> *I came here because I thought I liked the brewery.…There are good and bad people everywhere.…We must work together to see that the goodness comes out over the bad. There are whites and blacks who say you should hire black people, but I'm the President of this company and nobody is going to tell me how to run it.*

Mack's performance at the press conference, along with many meetings with the locals, worked to convince the Oshkosh community to support the brewery under his ownership. Local sales rebounded, and community investors even bought stock to help Mack complete the purchase of the brewery.

The ribbon-cutting ceremony to commemorate the change in ownership at Peoples was held on October 10, 1970. Wanting the company's beer to be the beer of Black culture, Mack embarked on an aggressive and expensive campaign to reach large urban markets such as Chicago and Memphis. But unfortunately, he just couldn't crack the market: Blacks were not buying his beer. He was quoted in the *Milwaukee Star*, a Black newspaper, as saying, "Whites are saying they don't want no nigger beer, and I don't know what the Blacks are doing." Mack's wife, Pearl, in a later interview said about the issue:

> *The culture* [in the late 1960s] *was that the Caucasian race could do better for you than you could do for yourself....A lot of times we didn't support each other, we still don't support each other the way we should.*

By November 1972, Mack's time was up: he had failed to penetrate the new markets, and the first of the SBA loan payments was coming due. He had to lay off staff, and his time at Peoples was effectively over. Mack lived in Oshkosh up until 1982. After the brewery closed and was torn down, he worked as an insurance agent for New York Life. He died on February 4, 2019, at the ripe old age of eighty-eight.

As of August 2020, the public can once again get its hand on Peoples beer. The Sacramento-based Black-owned brewery Oak Park Brewing (one of the owners is former NBA player and mayor Kevin Johnson) bought the rights to the original recipe and started producing it again. Mack's beer lives on.

CHAPTER 3

"BROTHER BOOTSIE"

THE CARTOONS OF OLLIE HARRINGTON

Reproduced throughout this book are just a few of the many *Bootsie* cartoons created by Oliver Wendell "Ollie" Harrington (1912–1995). From the 1930s through to the 1960s, Ollie's cartoons appeared as "strident denunciations of Jim Crow racism in the pages of such Black newspapers as the *Amsterdam News*, *Chicago Defender*, *Pittsburgh Courier* and others." I would love to say that it was my original idea to include these wonderful cartoons in the book, but on the real, it's been done before. In his towering 1965 book *Alcohol and the Negro: Explosive Issues*, John R. Larkins uses these same reproductions.

Bootsie made his first appearance in a cartoon called "Dark Laughter" in the December 28, 1935 edition of Harlem's *Amsterdam News*. That first cartoon shows Bootsie and a friend (later to be named Stewmeat) at the counter in a liquor store where only expensive imported liquor is sold. While Bootsie stands quietly by, his friend speaks for both of them: "Naw, Mister. Me an' Bootsie jus' wants some plain corn." As explained by Brian Dolinar in his work on Harrington published by the American Humor Studies Association:

> *After prohibition, many still brewed their own basement concoctions. Amidst the Depression, when blacks in Harlem had little extra money to spend, Bootsie and his unnamed friend only want cheap but potent corn liquor.*

Bootsie by Ollie Harrington, April 9, 1966. *From the* Pittsburgh Courier *Archives.*

The best way to describe the Bootsie character (for me, at least) is through a contemporary explanation provided to the people who followed him. This article is from the Saturday, February 9, 1952 *Pittsburgh Courier*:

> *"Bootsie" is the personification of the American urban Negro of the middle Twentieth Century.* [He] *is a composite of humor, the nostalgia, the sophistication, the weaknesses and the strengths of the man of color of his times.*
>
> *When you look at a "Bootsie" cartoon, you can start with an expectation of something which will cast a light on another facet of the complex character which the American colored man has developed out of the warp and woof of life in these times…in these parts…for guys whose ancestors experienced and survived generous applications of the tarbrush. "Bootsie" is strictly "your folks"…transplanted from country to town. "Bootsie" is a man of parts.…He lives by his wits…combining all the cunning naivete of the country bumpkin with the brittle crust of the "hepped" cat of the big-town who knows his way around. The result is one of the most interesting "characters" on the current American scene.*
>
> *He's Funny*
>
> *"Bootsie" is the technicolored Falstaff of present-day American letters. He is a man with a difference. He's Funny. He lends a laugh. He lets loose a shadowy sliver of light into the dark places of darksome "Darktown."*
>
> *But just in case you may be one of those "occasional" readers…*[of] *Tan Town publications who don't know "Bootsie"…suppose we take time to arrange an introduction. "Bootsie" is that Negroid cartoon character whose visage is seen weekly in the* Courier, *the world's best Negro-presented newspaper. "Bootsie's" "papa" is that inimitable humorist, Ollie Harrington.*

The cartoons I have chosen for this book all are drinking themed, but Harrington's vast body of work covers the human experience. A big thanks goes out to the *New Pittsburgh Courier* for granting me the rights to reproduce these images.

CHAPTER 4

BERTIE "BIRDIE" BROWN

BADASS MONTANA MOONSHINER

My life is all misery when I cannot get my booze
My life is all misery when I cannot get my booze
I can't live without my liquor, gotta have the booze to cure these blues
—Ma Rainey, "Blues and Booze," 1924

Originally from Missouri, Bertie (or Birdie—newspapers identified her as both) Brown showed up in Montana in 1891. She settled first in the Lewistown area and then, in 1913, along Brickyard Creek. She was one of the very few Black women homesteaders in the state. After a successful effort led by the Woman's Christian Temperance Union (WCTU), a state referendum to prohibit the sale of alcohol was passed in November 1916. The law went into effect in 1918. With that, Montana was a dry state (a full year before it was followed by the rest of the nation). But Bertie had other ideas. She first appeared in the *Fergus County Argus* on July 28, 1922:

> *HAS FINE STILL*
>
> *Bertie Brown, a colored woman, was arrested by Deputy Sheriff Bill Ryan on a charge of having in her possession a still used for manufacture of moonshine. The still was taken, along with the woman, and both were in Justice of the Peace Fred Skalicky's court. The defendant pleaded guilty and a fine of $150 was imposed and paid. The still is considered by the officers as the finest one yet seized. It is estimated that it would cost $200 to duplicate it. The defendant seemed to take considerable pride in the shining apparatus and directed attention to the fact that it was clean and in perfect condition.*

Bertie was now a convicted moonshiner, and according to the locals, she produced some of the safest and "best moonshine in the country." After the arrest, she kept her operation low profile and stayed clean during most of the Prohibition era, but she got pinched again in May 1933, this time by a federal prohibition investigator. On May 9, 1993, the *Montana Record-Herald* published an article titled "Four Stills Taken by Federal Agents" and, about Bertie, reported, "A 40-gallon still was seized when Bertie Brown was arrested near Gilt Edge along with six 52 gallon barrels and 300 gallons of corn and sugar."

If the six barrels were full of moonshine, they would have amounted to roughly 1,500 750-milliliter bottles' worth. That's a lot of hooch! If Bertie could have stayed under the radar for just a few more months, until federal repeal of Prohibition arrived in December 1933, perhaps her moonshine operation would have been left untouched by the local law enforcement officers and tragedy could have been averted. Her still was seized on a Tuesday, and she was dead by Saturday. The May 14, 1933 *Lewistown Democrat-News* reported that Bertie died from burns received:

> *At her place Saturday night through an explosion of gasoline that she was using in connection with some cleaning. The burns extended over several parts of the body, but were particularly severe on top of the head, where the burning was so deep that it affected the brain tissue. The woman remained conscious and up to a very short time before her death was conscious and talked rationally.*

In the last few hours of her life, Bertie let it be known that she wanted someone to find and take care of her beloved cat. Unfortunately, the cat was never found. In a few modern accounts of the story, she died while cooking up one last batch of "shine" when her still exploded in her face. Did she have more than one still, since one was seized just a few days prior? Or was it just a "gasoline stove explosion" like most papers reported at the time? The May 14, 1933 article concluded:

> *Birdie Brown was quite widely known, especially in the Gilt Edge district where she had resided for so long. She took great pride in her little ranch home, always keeping it spic and span. She was generally liked and all of her friends will regret to learn of her passing.*

In 2020, two Black women (Dia Simms and Erin Harris) became partial owners of Saint Liberty Whiskey. They are both veterans of Combs Enterprises and played prominent roles in the meteoric rise of Diddy's alcohol brands such as Cîroc vodka (see chapter 9). "In an effort to highlight the history of the Prohibition era that paved the way for women in the wine and spirits industry," Saint Liberty Whiskey makes a bourbon that bears Bertie's name: Bertie's Bear Gulch Bourbon. Former NBA player Alan Henderson's Henderson Spirits Group also gives a nod to Bertie, offering both Birdie Brown Plain Hooch and Birdie Brown Straight Wheat Whiskey. With these, Bertie's spirit lives on.

CHAPTER 5

COLORED MEN BEHIND THE BAR

A BRIEF LOOK AT SOME EARLY BARTENDERS

I said, "Hey Bartender
Hey man, looka here
Draw one, draw two
Draw three four glasses of beer"
—Floyd Dixon, "Hey Bartender," 1955

An *Evening Star* article dated March 26, 1903, states: "In the olden times there were a great many colored men who stood behind the bar in this community [Washington, D.C.], and as a rule, they were polite, attentive and competent." For this chapter, I had plenty of candidates to choose from but decided to highlight three: Cato Alexander (New York City), John Dabney (Richmond, Virginia) and Tom Bullock (who was originally from Louisville, Kentucky, but became famous working in St. Louis, Missouri). The Black bartender organization called the Mixologist Club, formed in Washington, D.C., at the turn of the twentieth century, is also mentioned.

CATO ALEXANDER

Pretty much everything one needs to know about Cato Alexander, perhaps the first celebrity bartender, is contained in his February 17, 1858 obituary from the *New York Daily Herald*:

BOOTSIE **By OLLIE HARRINGTON**

"Aw, Bootsie, whyn't 'choo go on home? Man, if I let you have another'n you'd be the first cullud man to go into orbit!"

Bootsie by Ollie Harrington, June 3, 1961. *From the* Pittsburgh Courier *Archives*.

DEATH OF CATO OF "THE ROAD"

Among the obituary notices in the paper today is one of the death of a person somewhat celebrated in his day and generation. Cato Alexander, a colored man, has just departed this life, at the age of 77 years. To most old knickerbockers, especially to those who sowed their "wild oats" five and twenty years ago, this patriarch among negroes of this city was as well known and as much respected as anyone in his class ever was. Cato Alexander, in other words, held much the same rank in the sporting world as Downing does now among the oyster eating and Newport frequenting merchants.

The Downing mentioned above is one Thomas Downing. He was a Black Virginian who was born free, moved to New York City and opened an oyster bar that became an empire. With a six-cent "all you can eat oysters" deal called the Canal Street Plan, his was the place to be between 1830 and 1860. Now back to Cato's obit:

Cato had a much more venerable look than Downing, his hair looking exactly like white wool, while his manners were courtly and of the old school. Unlike Downing also, Cato never dabbled much in politics, or had troubles with anybody, but stuck to his business and made a fortune.

Cato Alexander was a resident of New York nearly all his life. In the early days he was a slave, but obtained his freedom with others by the legislation of States.

In 1798, Cato was freed from slavery in New York under the Gradual Abolition of Slavery Act, which provided for gradual emancipation of enslaved people without making slavery illegal. Back to the obit:

He was here in the days when Gen. Washington was in this city, and loved in his old age to tell over and over again the times that he had waited upon that great man, how he had helped him to mount and dismount his horse, and many other things, which, done in connexion with illustrious persons, wonderfully increases the pride of a darkey. Cato seemed to have a peculiar gift [for] *hotel keeping. His larder was of the best, and his liquors were the boast of connoisseurs.*

After many changes and experiences as a host of public inns, Cato took a place out "on the road," opposite the shot tower. Although the locality is not now out of the city, in the days of Cato's glory and prosperity it was a drive of several miles to his resort. Then there was but one public road fit for fast driving, and its terminus was Cato's.

Cato's eponymous place, Cato's Tavern, was a two-story building at, roughly, East Fifty-Fourth and Second Avenue (the layout of the streets and avenues changed a bit as the city expanded). The "shot tower" mentioned was owned by George Youle, who built it in 1823 to manufacture lead shot that was used as ammunition. The public road for "fast driving" was the Eastern Post Road. Okay, back to the obit:

> *Everybody went there. It was the rage and the fashion. His suppers were proverbial for excellence, and in sleighing times the fathers and mothers of the present generation carried on many of their flirtations in the parlor of this then popular negro's house.*
>
> *Cato's prosperity increased with time. He was purported to have amassed a fortune. There must have occurred a crisis about this time—for the very* [White] *man—the Young America of that day, who made Cato rich by their lavish patronage, in turn became "hard up," and were accustomed to borrow first small and then larger sums. They were generally men of respectability and good families, and Cato was proud to be of service to them. But once embarked in the career of a money lender as well as money-maker, the old man commenced going down the hill. He has been heard to say that he lost $100,000* [about $3 million today] *in these friendly loans to "fast men" of his day. His place began to decline in favor; its reputation was on the wane. Old friends deserted it, while new ones could not be retained, and were diverted to more ambitious places of resort which began to spring up in the suburbs of the city.*
>
> *Cato lingered in his old place for a number of years. The road which passed by it was changed to another direction, and this made everything around it look still more deserted. He afterwards became involved, and his old house was sold. Cato was now almost too old to commence life anew, but he still made several unsuccessful attempts. His last effort was to open an oyster saloon in Broadway, near the Metropolitan Holtel. His familiar name, associated with so many recollections of the frolics of the past, drew to his place a small share of custom. The "old fogies" were often to be met in Cato's cellar, discoursing freely with him about the superior enjoyments of their younger days*—laudatores temporis acti [one who praises past times] *as compared to the present. In a short time, Cato gave up his* [oyster] *place and his name was not heard, nor his person seen in Broadway after that time. He had outlived everything but the memories of his early triumphs and success, and, relinquishing all hope of ever retrieving his fortunes, he retired to Church Street—the resort only of negros and the*

> *lower and more degraded classes of whites—where he died, and whence his funeral will be solemnized to-morrow.*

In the 1850s, Church Street in lower Manhattan was known as Black Broadway and was infamous for its prostitution, dance halls and gambling houses.

WHAT'S YOURS, GENTLEMEN?: THE MIXOLOGIST CLUB OF D.C., 1900

The November 10, 1900 edition of the *Colored American* reported:

> *The art of mixing liquors has come to be a highly respectable and profitable calling and men of excellent repute are found in its ranks. To protect the better grade of workman from the shiftless and unreliable, and to stimulate a broader spirit of fraternity an organization was found necessary.*

That organization was called the Mixologist Club and was established in Washington, D.C., in 1898. In the above-quoted article, the club's annual ball was announced, along with some facts about its officers. Robert R. Bowie, president, led the officers of the club, who were "well known to Washington 'men about town.'" Bowie was described as

> *of fine physique, manly bearing and dignified mien, he is a commanding figure in a crowd, and this, with an acknowledged executive ability, gives him a clear title to leadership bestowed upon him by an admiring constituency.*

The article went on to describe the club's membership:

> *As its name indicates, it is made up principally of the very useful gentlemen who tickle the popular palate with artistic combinations of the "fluid that cheers" and who are wont to talk entertainingly of the weather, the drama, the ring, the track, or politics while shoveling in the cracked ice or putting the finishing touches upon a "Mamie Taylor," a "Manhattan" or a "Rickey."*

The Mamie Taylor was a popular pre-Prohibition cocktail that consisted of scotch, lime juice and ginger beer with a garnish of either a lemon or lime. The Rickey, created at a Washington, D.C. bar in the 1880s, is a highball made from bourbon or gin, lime juice and carbonated water.

JOHN DABNEY AND THE ROYAL MINT JULEP, 1860

In October 1860, the nineteen-year-old Prince of Wales, who much later became King Edward VII (yes, the current King Charles's great-great-grandfather), found himself in Richmond, Virginia. A 1951 newspaper article about the visit, which took place ninety years earlier, reported that the prince's

> *most enjoyable experience is said to have been not the historical explanations and hospitable companionship of Governor Letcher, but the first taste of a mint julep mixed by a Negro of much local fame.*

That locally famous Negro was one John Dabney, a renowned restaurateur who made Richmond his home. Born around 1824 in Hanover Junction (now Doswell, Virginia), as a child, he achieved some acclaim as a jockey. Once he grew too large to race competitively, he became a waiter. Eventually he made his way to Richmond and became the head bartender at the old St. Charles Hotel, which was located at Fifteenth and Main Streets. After he left the St. Charles, John worked at the Ballard and Exchange Hotel, and his fame as a bartender spread. It was there that John served the Prince of Wales his first mint julep.

When the prince ascended the throne in 1901, the *Daily Times* of Richmond published an article about the prince's long-ago visit to the city:

> *HIS FIRST MINT JULEP*
>
> *One of the traditions of the Exchange was that it was here that the Prince first made the acquaintance of a mint julep, and in this connection it is a matter of record that John Dabney, the barkeeper at the Exchange, received for this mint julep five five-dollar gold pieces. John, it would appear, viewed life from a commercial, rather than a sentimental vantage ground, for he at once sold his five-dollar gold pieces for fifteen or twenty dollars each, thus securing for his julep some eighty or a hundred dollars. This probably hold the record for mint juleps.*

According to another account of the incident, John said about the payment, "My Lor,' I'd make them [juleps] every minute of the day for that!" It was also reported that "the silver cup from which the young heir to the throne drank this beverage is still preserved...as a relic of great value and interest." I wonder where that cup is now.

Between the 1860s and 1890s, John spent his summers at various Virginia watering places: Greenbrier, White Sulphur, Sweet Chalybeate, Alleghany and Old Sweet Springs. According to one account of his time in western Virginia:

> *A former Richmond belle, who spent her summer at the White Sulphur, remembers how John Dabney served guests on the veranda of the old White Sulphur Springs Hotel with his famous juleps, bringing them up the circular stairs which led from the bar below.*

On June 7, 1900, at the age of about seventy-five, John died at his home in Richmond. In an article from 1907, he was remembered:

> *He unquestionably was a negro of the most artistic and aristocratic proclivities, like John Dabney of old Sweet Springs fame, with all these good qualities which are to be won by constant association for generations with the proudest and best of Old Virginia institutions and old Virginia families. He was no common negro, for even down to this day the ordinary negro palate has never learned to appreciate the mint julep, and common negroes and other unappreciative sneeringly refer to it as "grass and whisky." The mint julep is a typical drink of the higher civilization, the development and the refinement of patrician tastes in stimulants alcoholic.*

TOM BULLOCK

The first time I ever heard of Tom Bullock was at the Evan Williams Ideal Bartender Experience in Louisville. There, Tom, portrayed by George Harris, ushered our group into a dark and cozy speakeasy and sat us around his bar. He made us a few drinks and recounted some of his history—all while never breaking character. (He did break character at the very end, when I gave him a copy of my first book, about pre-Prohibition whiskey guys in Washington, D.C.)

In 1917, Tom published a book containing 174 cocktail recipes acquired over his lifetime of bartending. Given that nationwide Prohibition was on the horizon, his timing could not have been worse. The introduction of the book reads:

> *Is it any wonder that mankind stands open mouthed before the bartender, considering the mysteries and marvels of an art that border on magic?*

> *The recipes in this book have been composed and collected, tried and tested, in a quarter-century of experience by Tom Bullock of the St. Louis Country Club.*

Tom was born in Louisville circa 1872. He started out as a bellboy but eventually found his way behind the bar, first at the Pendennis Club in Louisville before ending up at the St. Louis Country Club. In his book, he documents many colorful concoctions. Here are few of my favorites:

Bizzy Izzy High Ball

Drop 1 piece of Ice into a Highball glass.
2 dashes lemon juice.
2 teaspoonfuls of Pineapple Syrup.
½ jigger of Sherry Wine.
½ jigger of Rye or Bourbon Whiskey.

Free Love Cocktail

Lump Ice.
Use Shaker.
½ of the white of 1 Egg.
3 dashes Anisette,
1 jigger of Old Tom Gin.
1 pony fresh Cream.
Shake well, serve in cocktail glass.

Mint Julep, Kentucky Style

Use a large Silver Mug.
Dissolve one lump of Sugar in one-half pony of water.
Fill mug with Fine Ice.
Two jiggers of Old Bourbon Whiskey.
Stir well; add one bouquet of Mint and server.
Be careful and not bruise the Mint.

Today, former NBA player Alan Henderson and his Henderson Spirits Group offer two homages to Bullock's memory, a Burnt Orange Bourbon and an Old Tom Gin.

CHAPTER 6

MILKING AND MURDER IN ST. LOUIS

MEET JACK'S NEPHEW LEM MOTLOW

The whole trouble grew out of the insolence and verbal and physical attacks of the negro Pullman porter who swore on the witness stand that he belongs to a society whose object and demand is for social equality for whites and blacks.
—Lem Motlow, owner of Jack Daniel's, 1924

Unless you live under a rock, you know about how Uncle Nearest and his kin were instrumental in the whole Jasper Newton "Jack" Daniel whiskey story. (Shout-out to Fawn Weaver and her book *Love and Whiskey*.) But did you know that Jack's nephew, Lemuel "Lem" Oscar Motlow, who ran the company after Jack's death from 1907 until 1947, was involved in two of the most notorious court cases that took place in the 1920s? You wouldn't know it from the Jack Daniel's media site, which, in covering Lem's time in charge, says, in pertinent part:

> *Lem was a very good businessman, and he was known to be a fair and generous man. When Prohibition closed all the distilleries, Lem went into the mule business and started a mule auction.*

Let's take a closer look at the "fair and generous" Lem and the two court cases, one involving the breakup of one of largest bootlegging operations in the Midwest and the other involving Lem killing a man and getting out of the charges by blaming a Black man.

MILKING WHISKEY

Tennessee went dry in 1910, and Lem moved his distillery operations to St. Louis, Missouri; Birmingham, Alabama; and Cincinnati, Ohio. (This was when, back in Lynchburg, Tennessee, he was setting up his mule trading outpost). When Prohibition went nationwide in the 1920s, distilled liquors already had to be stored in bonded warehouses under federal supervision. According to the Jack Daniel's website's "Our Story" section on Prohibition, "[Motlow couldn't] sell his supply of whiskey, so he [stored] it in warehouses in Birmingham, Cincinnati, and St. Louis. For several years, a whole lot of good whiskey [wound] up doing a whole lot of nothing." It turns out that in the St. Louis warehouse at 3960 Duncan Avenue, where 896 barrels of his whiskey were kept, that whiskey did indeed do more than a whole lot of nothing. By 1923, a complicated conspiracy had been hatched to profit off that whiskey.

George Remus, the so-called King of the Bootleggers, was one of the lead coconspirators and the brains behind the plan to tap the barrels, remove the whiskey slowly so as to not alert the authorities, replace it with a poor grade alcohol diluted with water and sell the siphoned-off Jack Daniel's on the black market. Step one of the conspiracy was for the conspirators to buy Lem's supply of whiskey at the Duncan Avenue warehouse. Using a dummy corporation, a $125,000 check was issued to purchase the stock, and a contract was signed on June 26, 1923. This made the purchase appear completely legal, as the whiskey remained bonded and under government inspection.

A number of coconspirators were planted inside the warehouse, and an electric pump and 150 feet of hidden hose were installed. The hose ran into an adjacent parking garage, where barrel-filled trucks waited for the siphoned whiskey. These trucks would fan out, and the whiskey would be released into the black market. This process was known as milking. Remus's master plan called for removing the whiskey slowly and replacing it with small amounts of water and alcohol, which would initially be undetectable by taste or proof test. Each barrel contained forty gallons of whiskey, and the plan called for removing just six gallons from each of the 896 barrels; this would give the conspirators five thousand gallons to sell immediately. They would add enough water and alcohol to bring each barrel up to proof without ruining what whiskey remained. Knowing that the barrels were scheduled to be tested in December and would be found up to snuff, the conspirators could then tap from the barrels again to avoid detection.

Barrels of confiscated liquor. *Library of Congress.*

It was a good plan. Too bad they didn't stick to it. This is what happened: the low-level conspirators on the ground wanted to get the operation done in one fell swoop. So beginning in August 1923, they began milking the barrels of all their contents (thirty thousand gallons' worth) and filling the empty barrels with the water and alcohol mixture, which would likely pass the proof test but fail the taste or smell test spectacularly should a federal inspector choose to conduct them. The low-level guys thought they had the taste/smell angle covered in that their plants who worked in the warehouse were given the task of making sure the federal gauger (whose job it was to inspect the contents of the barrels periodically) be given access to only one lone, undiluted barrel of whiskey. This barrel was marked and its location made known to the plants. That way, the theory went, when the gauger showed up and wanted a taste, he'd be given a taste from that one barrel, be satisfied and not taste any other barrels.

Apparently, the low-level conspirators did not get the memo that the federal gauger (one Charles Barlow) had changed his scheduled inspection date and time, and none of the plants were on hand at the warehouse when he arrived. The night watchman on duty (who was not on the take) let Barlow sample a random barrel he'd selected, and the gauger got a mouthful of foul water mixed with low-grade alcohol. With that, the jig was up. The government now knew that the whiskey had been milked and was circulating on the black market. The bootlegged Jack Daniel's was soon turning up all over the Midwest: Ohio, Illinois, Indiana and Missouri. Once Remus caught wind of what happened, he was pissed that (1) they hadn't followed his careful plan and (2) he'd been cut out of some of the profits. A federal investigation was underway, and Remus started cooperating with it.

MURDER WAS THE CASE

Lem was one of the seventeen individuals indicted on federal bootlegging charges, and on the morning of March 17, 1924, he appeared in a downtown St. Louis courthouse in the case that would come to be known as *United States v. Motlow*. That night, on the train home to Tennessee, he shot and killed a man. The best way to tell this story is through contemporary newspaper articles written about the trial. From the December 10, 1924 *St. Louis Star and Times*:

> *A record crowd filled every available inch of space in Circuit Judge Hamilton's court to hear the final arguments of nine lawyers* [two for the state and seven for Lem] *participating in the trial of Lem Motlow, Lynchburg, Tenn., millionaire mule raiser and former distiller, charged with murder of Clarence T. Pullis, Kirkwood, Pullman Conductor.*
>
> *Pullis* [a White man] *was shot on the night of last March 17 in his car, which was attached to an L&N* [Louisville & Nashville] *train entering the tunnel leading to Eads Bridge. He died the following day in an East St. Louis hospital. Motlow contended he fired in self-defense, after an attack by Ed Wallis, negro porter, and one of the bullets hit Pullis by accident.*

The December 5, 1924 *St. Louis Star and Times* provided a detailed account from Wallis's testimony about what he recalled happening:

> *Wallis told of having first seen Motlow coming through the gates at Union Station at 8:30pm, an hour and six minutes before leaving time.*
>
> *"I was standing at the steps of my car when Motlow came up and asked him for his ticket," said Wallis. He said he had none and I told him to see Pullis who was at the table sorting Pullman tickets.*

> *Motlow started towards the gates after he had seen Pullis, as if to go into the station and get a ticket. He was almost to the gates when he turned around and came back shouting at me, "Lower three"* [indicating the berth that was supposedly his]. *He told me to change the berth around so he could sleep with his feet towards the engine instead of his head.*
>
> *He got in and I went with him. I fixed his berth and he gave me a quarter tip.* [Later, on the train,] *I started at Section 12 coming up the aisle towards Motlow. I was about twelve feet away when Pullis came in and asked Motlow for his ticket.*
>
> *Motlow said, I have no damn ticket, and I heard Pullis tell him to keep quiet and sit down….Motlow looked around at Pullis and me and said to Pullis, "Where did you get that nigger?" Calling me a name. Pullis tried to pacify him saying, "Sit down Mr. Motlow, Sit down."*
>
> *I said to Pullis, "You better stop that man abusing me or I'll get off this car." I heard Motlow say, "I was raised with niggers." Then he jumped up. I was standing behind Pullis and Motlow reached over Pullis' shoulder and hit me in the left eye.*
>
> *I told Pullis to put him to bed and Motlow was sitting down then got up. Both he and Pullis were facing me and about three feet away from me. Motlow reached into his pocket with his right hand and drew a pistol. He fired one shot, which struck Pullis in the side and Pullis fell. I grabbed Motlow's wrist and tussled with him, the gun going off again while I had ahold of him. I stumbled over Pullis who was on the floor then I grappled with Motlow. I was trying to restrain him from shooting me. When the gun went off during the struggle, the bullet grazed my left hand and passed through my coat tail.*

Another witness, when asked if Motlow was drunk, replied, "He sure was." The December 9, 1924 edition of the *St. Louis Post-Dispatch* detailed Motlow's version of the incident. The article reported that Motlow "told a story remarkably elastic in some important details, but unvarying in one difficult point—the assertion that he did not see Pullis near him when he fired the shot that killed the conductor."

> *He admitted drinking whisky—two drinks, from teacups which were "pretty well filled"—and he said he was "feeling" the drinks "a right smart" when he got on the train. His story on direct examination of the actual shooting did not admit the purposeful use of his revolver: "I reached for my gun, and I pulled it out and around and someone seized my hand*

> *and the gun was fired twice. I don't remember then I was unconscious, but when I came to, I was lying in the aisle of the car."*

Regarding the presence of Pullis in the car, the article detailed Motlow's testimony:

> *Motlow declared he did not see conductor Pullis at any time within the car, and that he was not aware when he fired, that Pullis was anywhere near him. He could not be brought to an admission that Pullis asked him for a ticket, or that there had been any meeting between them inside the car. The only person he saw was the "darky" and that individual had attacked him.*

Providing context about his "raised by niggers" comment, Motlow claimed to have said, "I have been raised by you niggers, and I am not used to being treated in that way." Motlow then explained, "Why there's one nigger on my place that nearly raised me but I'm a year older than he is. He calls me 'Lem' and I call him 'John.'" The article added, "The memory of boyhood seemed for an instant to lighten the horror of the trial for murder and Lem Motlow laughed."

Lem had quite the list of character witnesses testify on his behalf. One such witness was Austin Peay, who at the time was the sitting governor of the state of Tennessee. Regarding his testimony, a newspaper article reported:

> *Gov. Peay said that he has known Motlow for more than twenty years and that he was acquainted with the late Jack Daniels, who was Motlow's uncle. He said that it was the general understanding in Tennessee that when Daniels died, he left his estate to Motlow.…When asked* [by the prosecutor] *if he knew of the federal indictment against the defendant* [in the milking case], *he replied he did, and added, "People in my country are all, and I am sure, of the opinion that a man of Motlow's high integrity would never stoop so low as to be guilty of the dastardly offense of which the government has accused him."*
>
> [Motlow's lead attorney] *bitterly objected to the state being allowed to mention the federal indictment before the jury. "It is hideous to bring that into this case," he told the court.*

The closing arguments given by the attorneys on both sides must have been quite compelling. Unfortunately, we have only what the newspapers were able to capture. The prosecution summed up the matter thus:

Gentlemen here is what happened, and this what it amounts to, no matter how many flowery and eloquent speeches are made by the fiery orators from the Southland and silver tongued experts at law—a drunken man got on a train without a ticket, with a death-dealing pistol in pocket contrary to law and killed a man within a few minutes. That's all you can make out of it—murder—just the same as it was Cain's murder of Abel.

We contend that there is not one mitigating circumstance in the shooting, regardless of the fact that Motlow has called upon the whole state of Tennessee to come up here and try to save him. There is no distinction here between the millionaire defendant and the poor man.

First up of Lem's team of defense lawyers from Missouri and Tennessee (sort of a "dream team" of lawyers akin to those who represented O.J. Simpson) was Seth M. Walker of Nashville:

Attorney Walker began by telling of the historical friendship between Missourians and Tennesseans. Getting after some minutes to the case, he said, "No one regrets this occurrence more than does Lem Motlow. His heart goes out to the family of Mr. Pullis, who unfortunately lost his life. He was the victim of an accident, and the man who should be tried for his death is not Lem Motlow, but Ed Wallis."

Walker admitted Motlow had had a "few drinks," before adding, "It's no crime for a man to take a drink if it's a good one and he's lucky enough to have it."

One of Lem's St. Louis–based attorneys was a former circuit judge named Vital W. Garesche. Here is a snippet of his closing argument:

He referred to Wallis as "the black star witness for the state" describing him as a "human ourang-outang with reference to his physical strength" and said such a man could easily overcome a middle-aged man like Motlow.

Yep, that's right: Garesche likened Wallis to an orangutang—the great apes that are native to the rainforests of Indonesia.

Former Judge W.B. Lamb from Fayetteville, Tennessee, declared for the defense:

The trouble was due to Wallis' resentment at being called "nigger" by Motlow. After Motlow spoke to him as "nigger," the lawyer said, Wallis was heard by Motlow to mutter, "Nigger, nigger" in resentment.

MOTLOW AND HIS SEVEN LAWYERS AT MURDER TRIAL

Photo by Staff Photographer.

Wealthy Tennesseean in court here, charged with killing Clarence T. Pullis, Pullman conductor, photographed yesterday with his counsel. Seated, from left: Lem Motlow, Lynchburg, Tenn.; J. J. Bean, Lynchburg, Tenn., (just over Motlow's shoulder); Col. Frank P. Bond, Nashville, Tenn.; Former Circuit Judge Vital W. Garesche, St. Louis; Former Circuit Judge W. B. Lamb, Fayetteville, Tenn.; Patrick H. Cullen, St. Louis; Seth M. Walker, Nashville, Tenn.; Roy H. Parks, Lynchburg, Tenn. The two men with spectacles, standing in the rear, are Circuit Attorney Howard Sidener (left), and his assistant, Rowland L. Johnston, who are prosecuting Motlow.

"Motlow and his Seven Lawyers at Murder Trial," December 3, 1924. *From the* St. Louis Time and Star. *Photo restoration by Jason Hamacher.*

And finally we come to the seventy-three-year-old Colonel Frank P. Bond, who, one newspaper mentioned, "used the word nigger in all the numerous references he made to the negro race." The newspaper reported that Bond

> *made a thirty-five minute appeal in which he excoriated the state's witness, extolled those of the defense and devoted ten minutes to a eulogy of Andrew Jackson, a Tennessean, and Jackson's victory over the British at New Orleans. Bond's main argument was for white supremacy. He said the whites controlled civilization for 4,000 years and that "now the negro wants to share it."*
>
> *Bond continued, "There are two classes of niggers in this country. One is the kind that knows its place. These are niggers we love, care for, and protect. For these niggers we are ready to don our helmets and breast plates and go forth to battle. The other class demands racial and social equality. They want to intermarry with your daughters and mine. They shall not do it. They shall not do it.*

> *When the inevitable conflict comes we white men will stand together as one and stamp out this evil. The nigger Wallis is one of these nigger uplifters. He tells you he belongs to several uplift societies. He was insolent to Motlow because he thought Motlow was poor white trash because Motlow had on an old suit, was minus a necktie, and had no baggage. The human heart is not disclosed by raiment. The depth of the human soul is not gauged or measured by fine fabrics."*

The jurors took less than two hours to reach their verdict: they acquitted Lem on the first ballot. The jury foreman, Frederick Smith, was appointed to speak for all jurors when questioned by the press.

> *"We didn't believe the negro," Smith said, referring to the testimony of Wallis, who said that Motlow was drunk, and shot Pullis when the conductor tried to quiet him.*
>
> *"We believed," Smith continued "that there was a fight, and that Motlow was forced to defend himself. This was the opinion of us all, and there was little discussion among us. Everyone, in his first expression on the case, gave practically the same view."*

When asked about the effect of Colonel Bond's final argument, Smith replied, "Col. Bond certainly made an interesting and highly entertaining speech." It seemed that most of those in the courtroom were friendly toward Motlow, and people clapped their hands and cheered when the "not guilty" verdict was announced. Once the court was adjourned, Lem was free to express his thanks to the jury, and the newspaper reported:

> *First, his 11-year-old daughter, Mary, kissed him, as did Mrs. Motlow, and then they joined him in thanking the jurors. Some of the jurors entered into conversation with him, and there were hearty handshakes and back-slapping.*

On his return to Tennessee on December 13, 1924, Motlow made a prepared statement:

> *The whole trouble grew out of the insolence and verbal and physical attacks of the negro Pullman porter who swore on the witness stand that he belongs to a society whose object and demand is for social equality for whites and blacks.*

> *Public sentiment in St. Louis, which had been fanned to a white heat by the local press, was shown at the termination of the trial to have been changed as was evidenced by the applause from the great crowd gathered in the courtroom.*

The December 23, 1924 edition of the *St. Louis Post-Dispatch* ran an article titled, "Motlow Sends Turkey to Each Member of Jury: Letter of Thanks for Acquittal Verdict Accompanied Gift from Wealthy Tennessee Distiller." It read, in part:

> *A Tennessee turkey from Lem Motlow's Lynchburg homestead has been sent to each of the members of the St. Louis jury which acquitted the wealthy distiller, Dec. 10, of the charges of murder in the fatal shooting of Clarence T. Pullis….The wife of one* [jury] *member, when first asked about the matter, said no such gift had been received, and resented the inquiry, asking, "It* [would] *be a bribe wouldn't it?" When a second inquiry was made later, she said that the turkey had come, but refused to say whether it would be accepted.*

The milking case went to trial in Indianapolis in December 1925. Though a bunch of his coconspirators ended up with some jail time, Lem, of course, got off scot-free—again. Between 1939 and 1992, Jack Daniel's produced Lem Motlow's Tennessee Sour Mash Whiskey in a variety of sizes and proofs over the years. The label included Lem's visage and was produced in very limited quantities; it is said to be very expensive and hard to find.

CHAPTER 7

CAPTAIN CLARENCE WEBSTER

HERO AND BOOZE SMUGGLER

With the passage of the Twenty-First Amendment on December 5, 1933, Prohibition was repealed. The legal flow of alcohol into the United States was back on. The December 30, 1933 edition of the *Pittsburgh Courier* ran this headline: "Negro Captain Brings First Liquor Into the Port of New Orleans." The article identified Captain Clarence Webster as being from British Honduras (now Belize). "His trim motorship '*Laura*,'" hailing from the Port of Belize, was carrying 1,940 cases of whiskey, wines and cordials. The cargo was consigned under government seals, which were reportedly unbroken on arrival in New Orleans. The cargo was unloaded and removed to a bonded warehouse. In this instance, at least, Captain Webster was on the up and up.

It turns out that Captain Webster also had some history with bringing booze into the country illegally, during Prohibition. In enforcing the Volstead Act and attempting to keep liquor from seeping into the country from the south, the coastal counties of Mississippi (Jackson, Harrison and Hancock) had been forced to go it alone. In a January 1922 editorial from a Biloxi newspaper, the situation was described as follows:

> *Case upon case of liquor is brought in. They are found in the bays of the peninsula. Men's bodies come in upon the tide, and suspicion points strongly to illegal traffic.*
>
> *This business is not mere opposition to whiskey—it is opposition to Government and the supreme law.*

> *Inefficiency or inadequacy of means and money, makes a solemn, a tragic joke of the Government and its futile or weak efforts.*
>
> *It should cease to be a joke. People must awaken. Officers of city, county, and state must hold a conference. They must appeal for full federal co-operation in men and money.*

At this time, in 1922, Captain Webster was operating out of Biloxi on an oyster schooner named *Annie Mackie* and was involved in reporting one of the largest booze raids on the coast of Mississippi. As he recounted to the police, Webster met a liquor-laden vessel, later to be identified as the *Marina*, that was 108 days out from Batabanó, Cuba, with a cargo of liquor bound for Matamoras, Mexico. Failing to land in Matamoras, the *Marina* sailed to Tampico, where it lay for a month, still loaded and awaiting customers. Growing discouraged, the *Marina*'s captain set sail to return to Cuba, only to be hit with a storm. When Captain Webster came upon the *Marina*, it was lost and in dire need of reprovisioning. Webster directed the boat to Biloxi, where it could replenish its stores. He indicated that he couldn't provide immediate assistance as he and his crew "were engaged in the catch of oysters," and their provisions were also low. So Captain Webster returned to Biloxi when he was finished with his catch and obtained some provisions for the *Marina*. On his return to the ship:

> *We were informed of the shooting. A member of the crew told* [him] *that the men boarded their boat and first shot at their feet and then bound them to the deck. After investigating as to whether there were any firearms on the alleged carrier of contraband, and finding that there were none,* [the *Marina* crewman] *said that the men forced them (the crew of the ship) to load their cargo abord the smaller boat, which they told* [Webster] *was named* "Naomi."

The pirates took about 110 cases of liquor and took off into the night. It was later determined that the haul included "the finest brands of liquor, which was champagne, Old Taylor and other whiskies and French Cognac." Based on a tip from Webster, the authorities were able to track and then find the pirates. Thirty-six cases of contraband liquor were confiscated, and six of the Biloxi pirates were tried and convicted for their actions. As the January 16, 1922 edition of the *Daily Herald* put it: "Alleged Pirates Operate on Booze Boat Causing Biggest Raid in Years."

The U.S. Coast Guard cutter USS *Seneca* has chased and captured a rumrunner; Prohibition agents examine barrels on the rumrunner's boat. 1924. *Library of Congress.*

Three years after his historic delivery of "legal" liquor into New Orleans, Captain Webster, in 1936, was again in the headlines. This time, it was as a hero. The February 26, 1936 *Daily Mirror* recounted the story of how Captain Webster had been awarded the Royal Humane Society's Silver Medal at the recommendation of the governor of Honduras. The medal was awarded to individuals who put their own lives at risk to save the lives of others. Captain Webster saved the lives of 110 people when his ship *Laura* was wrecked on Utila Island, Honduras. As recorded in *Acts of Gallantry, Volume Two: Accounts of Deeds of Bravery in Saving Life 1871–1950 for Which the Royal Humane Society Awarded the Silver Medal and the Stanhope Gold Medal*:

> *Webster, Clarence G., Captain, Motor Vessel C.M. Laura, Case 53232*
>
> *The wooden Motor Vessel C.M. Laura, 75 tons net register, left Belize Honduras, on 14th March, 1935, with passengers, mostly women and children, and a crew of eight, bound for Utilla Island, Republic of Honduras.*

> *A strong north-westerly wind, accompanied by heavy rain squalls, sprang up during the night. Whilst running before the heavy following seas, the vessel grounded on the north coast of the island about 3:30 a.m. and in pitch darkness. The engines were reversed, but without result, the vessel remaining fast on the rocks with heavy seas breaking over her, causing her to pound heavily, with every likelihood of breaking up quickly.*
>
> *The searchlight was switched on and it was then discovered that her bows were about 60 feet off the low and rock bound coast and that there was considerable backwash of the 10 ft. high and jagged rocks. The lifeboat was smashed to splinters by the dispatch.*
>
> *Capt. Webster who was in the Chart Room when the vessel grounded, tried to quieten the frenzied passengers, and, seeing that none of the crew in the bows were making any attempt to get a line ashore, secured a line around his waist, dived overboard from the poop, swam amongst the rocks until able to reach the shore, where he experienced great difficulty in landing, due to the backwash and heavy seas, secured the line and then returned along it to supervise the landing of his passengers and crew.*
>
> *None of the passengers could be induced to make the attempt until Mr. McPherson Miller, himself a passenger, joined the Captain in the water, and between them the two men managed to land safely the whole of the passengers and crew, remaining in the water until the last was safely landed at daybreak. Capt. Webster was badly cut and bruised by contact with jagged rocks whilst swimming ashore. The vessel became a total wreck.*
>
> *Capt. Webster was awarded the Society's Silver Medal and Mr. McPherson Miller the Bronze Medal.*

Just over a year later, in 1936, as announced in the May 10 edition of the *Tampa Tribune* in an article titled "U.S. Holds Honduran Negro Sailor on Smuggling Charges," Captain Webster and his younger brother Cashmon were arrested in New Orleans for smuggling alcohol. Their motor vessel, the *Cisne*, operated between Tampa and New Orleans. Unfortunately for Cashmon, his arrest led to his immediate deportation—apparently, he had entered the country illegally. There is no record of how Captain Webster beat the charges, but he did live to sail another day.

Sadly, it was another brush with the sea a year later that cost Captain Webster his life. On June 15, 1937, the *Tampa Times* reported that the family of a missing man was imploring the British to search for a missing vessel, a 110-foot banana boat called the *Maloa*, as the U.S. Coast Guard had called off the search. The boat had left Tampa en route to Belize, Honduras, on

June 2. At the time of the last report from the *Maloa*, it was somewhere between Dry Tortugas and Cape San Antonio at the western tip of Cuba. The coast guard reported sighting a burning derelict about fifty-five miles southwest of Cuba on the Tampa–Belize route. Captain Webster was one of the ten souls on board the *Maloa* who so mysteriously disappeared.

CHAPTER 8

BLACK TEMPERANCE

BEDIMMED AND BEDIZZIED

> [Blacks] *rule our cities to-day, the saloon their palace, the toddy stick their sceptre. It is not fair that they should vote, nor is it fair that a plantation Negro who can neither read nor write, whose ideas are bounded by the fence of his own field and the price of his own mule, should be entrusted with the ballot. The Anglo-Saxon race will never submit to be dominated by the Negro so long as his altitude reaches no higher than the personal liberty of the saloon and the power of appreciating the amount of liquor that a dollar will buy.…Better whiskey and more of it has been the rallying cry of a great dark-faced mob in Southern localities where Local Option* [Prohibition] *was snowed under by the colored vote.*
>
> *—Frances Elizabeth Willard, president of the Woman's Christian Temperance Union, 1890, blaming Black voters for the failure of a Prohibition ballot measure in the South*

There is evidence of Black interest in temperance as early as 1788, when the Free African Society of Philadelphia refused membership to all drinkers. One of the first organized Black efforts against intemperance began around 1829 with the formation of the New Haven Temperance Society for the People of Color and the New York Temperance Society. In 1831, just over two hundred black Baltimoreans established a temperance society based on moral reform principles. It sought to counter the goal of the predominately White American Colonization Society (ACS) to send free Blacks to Africa as an alternative to emancipation. Formed in 1817, the ACS by 1822 had established a colony on the west coast of Africa that, in 1847, became the independent nation of Liberia. By 1867, the ACS had sent more than thirteen thousand emigrants to Liberia. In forming their temperance society, the Black Baltimoreans contented that the adoption of temperance and moral reform would prove the worthiness of the Black character.

JOHN BROWN RUSSWURM

Jamaican-born and the first Black man to graduate from Bowdoin College, Russwurm cofounded the newspaper *Freedom's Journal* on March 16, 1827, in New York City. The paper ceased publication after only 103 editions in April 1829, but at its peak, it had a distribution that spanned over eight hundred copies throughout eleven states and the District of Columbia. Russwurm embraced the goals of the ACS and saw his newspaper's popularity decline as many northern Blacks began to oppose its goals and he lost financial backing. Russwurm immigrated to Liberia in November 1829. He served as superintendent of public schools and editor of the *Liberia Herald* before becoming governor of Maryland County, Liberia, in 1836. He remained in that office until his death on June 9, 1851, at the age of fifty-two.

Russwurm was one of the authors responsible for this satirical musing on the evils of drink in the July 27, 1827 edition of *Freedom's Journal*:

> *THE DRUNKARD'S WILL*
>
> *O, beginning to be enfeebled in body and fearing I may soon be palsied in mind, and having entered on that course of intemperance from which I have not strength of mind to flee, and already feeling the evils resulting from it, which I have not resolution to avert, do make and publish this my last will and testament. Having been made in the image of my Creator, capable of rational enjoyment, of imparting happiness to others, and promoting the glory of God, I know and acknowledge my accountability; yet such is my fondness for sensual gratification, and my utter indisposition to resist temptation, that I give up myself entirely to intemperance and its associate vices, and make the following bequests:*
>
> *My property I give to dissipation, knowing it will soon fall into the hands of those who furnish me with ardent spirits.*
>
> *My reputation, already tottering on a sandy foundation, I give to destruction.*
>
> *I give my ability to be useful and happy in life, to annihilation.*

> *To my beloved wife, who has cheered me so far in the path of life, I give shame, poverty, and a broken heart.*
>
> *To each of my children I bequeath my example, and the inheritance of the shame of their father's character.*
>
> *Finally, I give my body to disease, misery and early dissolution, and my soul that can never die, to the disposal of that God, whose mercy I have abused, whose commands I have broken, and who has declared that no drunkard shall inherit the kingdom of heaven.*

By the late 1830s, the number of Black temperance organizations had expanded greatly. The Coloured American Convention Temperance Society was formed in 1831 with the intention of overseeing the efforts of local Black temperance societies and promoting cooperation with their White brothers. Eventually, there were twenty-three branches in eighteen cities, including Washington, D.C.; Philadelphia and Carlisle, Pennsylvania; New Haven, Hartford and Middletown, Connecticut; Boston, Massachusetts; and Princeton, New Jersey; Albany, Schenectady, Utica, Syracuse, Catskill, Poughkeepsie, Newburg, Troy and New York City, New York. Following the pattern established by White temperance groups, these Black branches first adopted a moderate temperance stance, pledging abstinence from only "ardent spirits," defined as strong liquors made from distillation, such as whiskey, brandy or gin. Indeed, in 1826, Lyman Beecher (yes, the father of Harriet Beecher Stowe, who later wrote *Uncle Tom's Cabin*) delivered his famous *Six Sermons on Intemperance* and had this to say about those who sell ardent spirits:

> *The vending of ardent spirits, in places licensed or unlicensed, is a tremendous evil.…The continued habit of dealing out ardent spirits, in various forms and mixtures leads also to frequent tasting, and tasting to drinking, and drinking to tippling, and tippling to drunkenness.*

Beecher, a Presbyterian minister, often used a verse from the Bible contained in the book of Habakkuk 2:15–16, which in the King James Version of the Bible reads:

> *Woe unto him that giveth his neighbor drink, that puttest thy bottle to him and makest him drunken also that thou mayest look on their nakedness!*
>
> *Thou art filled with shame for glory; drink thou also, and thy foreskin be uncovered: the cup of the Lord's right hand shall be turned unto thee, and shameful spewing shall be on thy glory.*

I mean, I don't even know where to begin with this. Nakedness, foreskin uncovering and shameful spewing—wow. Perhaps I should have paid more attention at Vacation Bible School?

By 1836, a shift away from moderate temperance to total abstinence had begun. Black leader J.W.C. Pennington resolved that his Connecticut State Temperance Society of Colored People should adopt total abstinence as part of its obligation to those who remained slaves. To Pennington, his fate and that of every free Black was inextricably linked to those in chains. The shift to total abstinence was pretty much complete by 1837. That year, it was reported that four thousand African Methodist Episcopal (AME) and African Methodist Episcopal Zion (AMEZ) ministers had abandoned consumption of all forms of alcohol.* Black leaders now stressed the theme of community survival as well as the connection between Black temperance and abolitionism. In the July 20, 1839 edition of the *Colored American*, a Black newspaper published in New York City from 1837 to 1842, an article titled "For the Colored American Means of Elevation—No. III Temperance" stated, "Slavery, intemperance, and immorality are the greatest curses of this nation. They go hand in hand. The prevalence of one of these vices is incidental to the existence of the other."

In the April 29, 1837 edition of the *Colored American* was published the "Annual Report of the Temperance Society of the People of Color in the City of Pittsburgh and vicinity." An excerpt reads:

> *Total Abstinence from all intoxicating drink.*
>
> *Intoxicating liquors have been banished from the house of almost every respectable family in our city. On entering the house of any respectable individual, at the present time, and to be presented with....It is considered disrespectable by all our intelligent and thinking people, to drink intoxicating liquors, or to be found in places where they are sold. The doctrine that they are useless, unwholesome and pernicious, as a common beverage, is understood and believed by nearly all. And it is hoped that the period is not distant when no individual can be found who will be so deluded as to admit one drop of this liquid poison, as a common beverage, between his lips.*

* The AMEZ denomination, whose structure, theology and culture are similar to the AME's, started around 1800 in New York City, while the AME denomination started around Philadelphia at about the same time.

> *Good News from Other Places*
> *From different parts of all the Free States we have heard the most cheering accounts of the success of the Temperance cause during the past year. In New England our brethren have acted most nobly. Besides forming many smaller Societies in the different large towns and cities, the people of Connecticut have formed what is styled the New England Temperance Society. When the moral energies of this refined and enlightened region are thus combined and concentrated, they will doubtless, under God, effect much good.*
>
> *In many parts of the middle States, our people are quite alive to the importance of the Temperance cause. Societies exist in nearly all the large towns and cities. And the number of members in many of them is quite large. Many public meetings have been held, and much has been done to push forward this good work.*
>
> *In several large towns and cities in the western States, Temperance societies exist among our people, some of which are large, and in a flourishing state. But the newness of the country, sparseness of the population, and cares and anxieties incident to new settlement, prevent, in many places, that attention to this important subject, which would otherwise be bestowed. It is hoped that this interesting region will ultimately become as famous for whatever is morally good, as it is for whatever is physically great.*
>
> *From some of the southern States, the land of our oppressed brethren, we have heard interesting news on the subject of Temperance during the past year. Many of our brethren in bondage are members of Temperance Societies. Though, in too many instances, deprived of almost every earthly means of moral instruction, yet the Most High has taught them by His Spirit, that it is wrong to drink intoxicating liquors. Cruel men have fastened upon them the yoke of the slave. They are conscious that although they are forced to be slaves of men, yet they may be, and in thousands of instances are, the freeman of the Lord.*

FREDERICK DOUGLASS'S 1846 TEMPERANCE ADDRESS

In his "Temperance and Anti-Slavery" address delivered in Paisley, Scotland, on March 30, 1846, Frederick Douglass did two things. First, he provided a firsthand account of how slaveholders used alcohol to control their slaves, and second, he gave an account of the horrid 1842 Philadelphia riot that was spurred in part by a White response to Black efforts to promote temperance. This is what Douglass had to say about the use of alcohol during slavery:

> *I have had some experience of intemperance as well as of slavery. In the Southern States, masters induce their slaves to drink whisky, in order to keep them from devising ways and means by which to obtain their freedom. In order to make a man a slave, it is necessary to silence or drown his mind. It is not the flesh that objects to being bound—it is the spirit. It is not the mere animal part—it is the immortal mind which distinguishes man from the brute creation. To blind his affections, it is necessary to bedim and bedizzy his understanding. In no other way can this be so well accomplished as by using ardent spirits! On Saturday evening, it is the custom of the slaveholder to give his slaves drink, and why? Because if they had time to think, if left to reflection on the sabbath day, they might devise means by which to obtain their liberty.*

Slaves were allowed to have alcohol at the discretion of the White slaveowner and only on his property. Alcohol was provided in great quantities, and drinking was encouraged at specific times, such as at the end of harvest and during the holidays, when the slaves had leisure time. A harrowing contemporary account of this practice is found in the June 6, 1845 edition of the *Liberator*, penned by a female correspondent:

> *The following sketch of the effects of the holidays which are granted to the slaves, is highly instructive, as revealing the arts of the slaveholder to make their victims disgusted with the idea of perpetual freedom.*
>
> *The days between Christmas and New Year's day are allowed as holidays; and, accordingly, we were not required to perform any labor, more than feed and take care of the stock. This time we regarded as our own, by the grace of our masters; and we therefore used or abused it nearly as we pleased.... It was deemed a disgrace not to get drunk at Christmas; and he was regarded as lazy indeed, who had not provided himself with the necessary means, during the year, to get whiskey enough to last him through Christmas.*
>
> *From what I know of the effect of these holidays upon the slave, I believe them to be among the most effective means of the slaveholder in keeping down the spirit of insurrection.... Their object seems to be, to disgust slaves with freedom, by plunging them into the lowest depths of dissipation. For instance, the slaveholder not only likes to see the slave drunk on his own accord, but will adopt various plans to make him drunk. One plan is, to make bets on their slaves, as to who can drink the most whiskey without getting drunk; and in this way they succeed in getting whole multitudes to drink to excess.*

About the 1841 riot in Philadelphia, Douglass said this:

> *To give you some idea of the strategy of this prejudice and passion against coloured people, I may state that they formed themselves into a temperance procession in Philadelphia, on the day which the legislature of this country had by a benevolent act awarded freedom to the negroes in the West Indian islands. They formed themselves into a procession with appropriate banners, but they had not proceeded up two streets before they were attacked by a reckless mob, their procession broken up, their banners destroyed, their houses and churches burned down, and the mob was backed up by the most respectable people in Philadelphia.*

The Lombard Street historical marker that commemorates this 1842 riot in what is now the Society Hill neighborhood of Philadelphia reads:

> *Here on August 1, 1842, an angry mob of whites attacked a parade celebrating Jamaican Emancipation Day. A riot ensued. African Americans were beaten and their houses looted. The riot lasted for 3 days. A local church and abolition meeting place were destroyed by fire.*

In a parade to celebrate the eighth anniversary of Jamaican emancipation, around 1,200 members of the Moyamensing Temperance Society marched in the hope of recruiting more members into the organization. They were attacked by an Irish mob on Fourth Street, and the marchers retaliated. At the time, in Philadelphia, Blacks and Irish immigrants lived in the same general vicinity, directly competed for the same unskilled jobs and housing and frequently clashed in trying to advance.

During the riots, the Irish mob burned down the Second African Presbyterian Church and the Smith Beneficial Hall on Lombard Street (where abolition lectures had been held). For two days, rioters ran amok throughout the Black community. Hundreds of Blacks fled the city to escape the rampaging mob that the city's police and militia either could not or would not control. Right after the riots ended, White political leaders ordered a brick building that had been used by the Blacks for temperance events to be torn down. The Whites believed that the building symbolized the social and economic progress of the Black community and would be used as a gathering place where further outbursts might be planned. Douglass later bitterly remarked that the Philadelphia mob represented White America's response to Black attempts at advancement:

"Almost every step he [the Black man] takes toward mental, moral, or social improvement is repulsed by the cold indifference or the active mob of the white."

EXCERPTS FROM BLACK NEWSPAPERS ON TEMPERANCE

With some of the money Douglass earned from his speaking tour of Great Britain and Ireland the previous year, he first published the abolitionist newspaper called the *North Star* on December 3, 1847, in Rochester, New York. The name of the paper paid homage to the fact that escaping slaves used the North Star in the night sky as a guide to freedom. Here are two interesting vignettes taken from the newspaper:

September 29, 1848
DEATH BY WHISKEY

At Indianapolis, Ind., the other day, one lad bantered another to drink all the liquor he could buy. He was taken up at this offer—whiskey and brandy were brought out, and the drinking commenced. Dose after dose was taken, until the drinking youth has swallowed about a quart! He then become insensible, and lingered about thirty-six hours, and died!

SCIENTIFIC DARKEY TRICK

The negroes of the West Indies have a method of stealing rum, which involves a principle of pneumatics. They take a bottle filled with water, invert it, and place the neck in the bung-hole of the barrel, so as to touch the liquor; the water being the heaviest, sinks into the liquor, leaving a vacuum in the bottle, which is then filled with the liquor forced up by the atmospheric pressure.

After all, there is a moral principle involved in the above, cant as it may appear. Those who are most oppressed and have the fewest privileges, are generally the most expert in schemes and tricks of cunning. The character is remarkable in the slaves of the South also, (sorry are we of the necessity of so disparaging woman as to say it, but upon the miserable heads of despotic men let the shame rest,) remarkable in females, so much so, that among men it has become proverbial that "Nothing can equal the cunning of woman." We repeat, that wherever there is oppression and tyrannical restriction, it compels a resort to schemes, tricks and cunning.

Continuing the focus on Black newspapers and their messaging on temperance themes, we next encounter the *Provincial Freeman*, the first Canadian weekly newspaper founded by an African American woman, named Mary Ann Shadd Cary. Born in Wilmington, Delaware, in 1823, she immigrated to Canada after passage of the Fugitive Slave Act of 1850. Her newspaper was published between 1853 and 1857. In one article from the June 13, 1857 edition, we encounter Dr. Hiram Cox, who published articles in a number of newspapers about the evils of alcohol from his perspective as chemical inspector of alcoholic liquors for Hamilton County, Ohio, where Cincinnati is the county seat.

> *DR. HIRAM COX, chemical inspector of alcoholic liquors, in Cincinnati, states, in an address to his fellow citizens, that during two years he has made 249 inspections of various kinds of liquors, and has found more than nine-tenths of them imitations, and a great portion of them poisonous concoctions. Of brandy, he does not believe there is one gallon of pure in a hundred gallons, the imitations having corn whiskey for a basis, and various poisonous acids for the condiment. Of wines not a gallon in a thousand purporting to do sherry, port sweet Malaga, &c., is pure, but they are made of water, sulphuric acid, alum, Guinea pepper, horse radish and many of them without a single drop of alcoholic spirit. Dr. Cox warrants there are not ten gallons of genuine port wine in Cincinnati. In his inspection of whiskey he has found only from 17 to 20 percent, of alcoholic spirits, when it should have 45 to 50, and some of it contains sulphuric acid enough in one quart to cut a hole in a man's stomach.*

Dr. Cox pops up again in the January 3, 1863 edition of the *Christian Recorder*, which is the oldest continuously published Black newspaper in the United States. Founded on July 1, 1852, it is the official newspaper of the AME Church. This time around, it is beer that is on Dr. Cox's mind:

> *DR. COX ON BEER*
>
> *There is "death in the pot" in anything and everything but water. Even beer, that has been lauded by my profession, is most pernicious on the system. I regret, and have regretted a thousand times, that scientific men should have made such an announcement, behind which erring men, without the ability to investigate, have taken shelter; and that, in consequence, men, women and children are drinking that which contaminates the system, produces a morbid derangement of all the glands and tissues, and transmits to their*

progeny a morbidly deranged, though finely formed, and sometimes an apparently healthy organism. Yet, when disease takes hold of the children of beer-drinking parents, they wilt down like Jonah's gourd, irrespective of the skill of the physicians and solicitude of the parents. I have been astonished at the difference presented by the same disease in the children of beer-drinking parents, and those who drink water—astonished to see how suddenly and easily the former succumb and die, compared with the latter. I have had a considerable amount of practice in beer-drinking neighborhoods, and what I state above are pathological facts of thirty years' standing. It is my experience, too, as a surgeon, that all diseases belonging to that department of my profession, are much more difficult of treatment in the beer-drinkers than even in whisky-topers; ulcers and sores of any kind are more unmanageable; fractured bones do not unite with equal facility; and I never saw an incised would heal by what surgeons call the first intention, in a beer-drinking subject. When a tendency to plethora exists, the beer-imbiber is always in danger of sudden death by apoplexy, or some other disease of the brain.

I have a great desire to see the glorious cause of Temperance take a high stand in this world of sin and sorrow; and old and feeble as I am, so intimately do I conceive it to be connected with religion, I profess that I am ready to spend and be spent in the service. If what I have said should be the means of redeeming one poor erring brother or sister, I am paid, and shall praise God in eternity for it.

HIRAM COX, Chemical Inspector of Liquor

Here is another curious blurb from the December 27, 1862 edition of the *Christian Recorder*:

WHISKY AND NEWSPAPERS

A glass of whisky is manufactured from perhaps a dozen grains of corn, the value of which is too small to be estimated. A pint of this mixture sells for one shilling, and it, of a good brand, is considered well worth the money. It is drunk in a minute or two—it fires the brain, sharpens the appetite, deranges and weakens the physical system. On the same sideboard upon which this pernicious beverage is served lies a newspaper. It is covered with half a million of types—it brings intelligence from the four quarters of the globe. The newspaper costs less than the glass of grog—the juice of a few grains of corn; but it is no less strange than true that there is a large portion of the community who think corn juice cheap and the newspaper dear.

TEMPERANCE IN THE SOUTH: "KEEP WHISKEY FROM THE NEGRO"

This slogan supposedly originated in Reconstruction times, according to a 1968 article in the *Journal of Negro History* by Dr. Charles Crowe. Crowe went on to detail how preachers in Atlanta circa 1906 whipped up prohibitionist thoughts:

> *In sermon after sermon* [Reverand Sam P.] *Jones stressed the special and intolerable evils which sprang from the consumption of alcohol by Negroes. The same subject was thoroughly discussed by Dr. John E. White, Pastor of the Second Baptist Church and commonly acknowledged dean of the city pulpit. The sermons and public statements of White and Jones inspired other ministers to imitate their example.... Civic and religious leaders argued that the black man's terrible biological craving for intoxicating beverages would compel the South to deprive him of whiskey by imitating the restrictive policies of the U.S. government toward the "inferior" peoples of the South Seas. In ante-bellum days, insisted the reformers, every plantation had been a prohibition island until the "license" of freedom made liquor "the most oppressive force" in black America. In brief, they demanded that whiskey be taken from the Negro to protect the black man from "relapse into animalism," the whites from Negro crime, and the South from the ever constant danger of race war.*

In the late 1890s, the group that called themselves the Committee of Fifty, made up of White businessmen and scholars, sought to investigate problems with the use and abuse of alcohol. In one of their works, they discussed what the temperance movement looked like in the South with regard to Blacks at the beginning of the twentieth century:

> *Of aggressive temperance work there is hardly any among the Southern Negroes. What is done to promote sobriety is done by preachers, who rarely institute vigorous temperance crusades. Prudence forbids them to attack the white man's saloon too directly. The attempts to form total abstinence societies and branches of the W.C.T.U.* [Woman's Christian Temperance Union] *have not been conspicuously successful. It is very doubtful, also, if the signing of pledges and other devices adopted by the churches prove effective. In the conception of the average uneducated Negro, morality is a thing quite apart from religion. He may be said to live two*

lives—a religious and an every-day life. The former is largely a life of emotion and excitement, and not of principle. Preaching abstinence is therefore not likely to lead to extensive practice. Local prohibition in the South has frequently been carried by Negro votes won over by the frenzied appeals of agitators; but through promises of more substantial rewards for the same Negro votes, prohibition has sometimes been defeated.

The better educated Negroes of the North particularly have taken up a more general and systematic temperance work, but as yet it has not assumed a very practical turn. Perhaps the race as a whole is not quite ripe for such efforts. At the present time, it is certainly burdened by weightier problems pressing for solution than the problem of intemperance.

In the August 12, 1907 edition of the *Daily Leaf Chronicle* of Clarksville, Tennessee, under the headline "Negro Bishop Takes Sensible Position," the author concluded that the "negro problem" had a lot to do with the White man's saloons. The bishop explained:

White men license a white man to run a saloon to sell liquor to Negroes. When they patronize the saloon, as they are expected to do, their baser instincts are aroused by the white man's liquor, under the influence of which they commit some crime. Immediately, they are arrested by a white man, and with or without a trial are condemned by white men and sentenced either to the penitentiary or to be hanged. But the trouble was originally not with the Negro, but the white man's saloon.

He called for an end to this aspect of the "Negro" problem and contended that the place to begin was Clarksville. "No man white or colored can afford to be left behind in this great move for the good of both races."

Booker T. Washington had this to say about temperance in the South in 1908:

I have read much in the northern papers about the prohibition movement in the South being based wholly upon a determination or desire to keep liquor away from the negroes and at the same time provide a way for the white people to get it. I have watched the prohibition movement carefully from its inception to the present time and I have seen nothing in the agitation in favor of the movement, nothing in the law itself, and nothing in the execution of the law that warrants any such conclusion. The prohibition movement is based upon a deep-seated desire to get rid of whisky in the interest of both races because of its hurtful economic and moral results. The prohibition sentiment is as strong in counties where there are practically no colored people as in the Black Belt counties.

FRANCES ELLEN WATKINS HARPER: TEMPERANCE LITERATURE

One of the best-known and most prolific Black writers of the nineteenth century was Frances Ellen Watkins Harper. She was a suffragist, abolitionist, poet and temperance advocate, among other things, all wrapped into one. She was born free in Baltimore on September 24, 1825, and her poems and novels were often serialized and reprinted in the Black periodicals of the day, such as the *Liberator*, the *Christian Recorder* and the *National Era*. Her works often invoked temperance themes. In one of her earliest poems with such a theme, as discussed in Doveanna Fulton's 2007 article in the journal *Legacy* about Harper titled "Sowing Seeds in an Untilled Field: Temperance and Race, Indeterminacy and Recovery in Frances E.W. Harper's Sowing and Reaping," she set the precedent for what would become the literary paradigm of temperance writing:

Frances Ellen Watkins. *Library of Congress.*

The deathbed scene of an intemperate character's loved one, the anticipated (yet often unfulfilled) arrival of the drunkard onto the death scene, and character descriptions with racially ambiguous physical markers.

We see all of these in Harper's work "The Drunkard's Child," from her second book, *Poems on Miscellaneous Subjects* (1854):

He stood beside his dying child,
With a dim and bloodshot eye;
They'd won him from the haunts of vice
To see his first-born die.
He came with a slow and staggering tread,

A vague, unmeaning stare,
And, reeling, clasped the clammy hand,
So deathly pale and fair.
In a dark and gloomy chamber,
Life ebbing fast away,
On a coarse and wretched pallet,
The dying sufferer lay:
A smile of recognition
Lit up the glazing eye;
"I'm very glad," it seemed to say,
"You've come to see me die."
That smile reached to his callous heart,
It sealed fountains stirred;
He tried to speak, but on his lips
Faltered and died each word.
And burning tears like rain
Poured down his bloated face,
Where guilt, remorse and shame
Had scathed, and left their trace.
"My father!" said the dying child,
(His voice was faint and low,)
"Oh! Clasp me closely to your heart,
And kiss me ere I go.
Bright angels beckon me away,
To the holy city fair—
Oh! Tell me, Father, ere I go,
Say, will you meet me there?"
He clasped him to his throbbing heart,
"I will! I will!" he said;
His pleading ceased—the father held
His first-born and his dead!
The marble brow, with golden curls,
Lay lifeless on his breast;
Like sunbeams on the distant clouds
Which line the gorgeous west.

In 1883, Harper, as a member of the Woman's Christian Temperance Union, held the position of "Superintendent of Work among Colored People in the North," a job in which she oversaw the formation of Black unions and

Black youth groups and the circulation of temperance literature. Perhaps she was recruited to the organization by the song "Let Us Help the Colored People," which the WCTU put out in 1880 with the explicit intention of recruiting Black women to its ranks. By the 1890s, Harper, frustrated with the National WCTU's appeasement of the racial agenda of its southern members, had been forced out of her leadership role in the organization.

It appears that Harper was caught in the crossfire of a dispute between Black anti-lynching activist Ida B. Wells and the WTCU's president, Frances Willard. In an 1890 article, Willard, commenting on the failure of a prohibition ballot measure in the South, squarely put the blame on Black voters (see the epigraph at the beginning of this chapter). Willard wrote:

> *I pity the Southerns, and I believe that the great mass of them are as conscientious, and kindly-intentioned toward the colored man, as an equal number of church members in the North.... The problem on their hands is immeasurable. The colored race multiplies like locust of Egypt. The grog shop is its centre of power.*

In 1894, both Willard and Wells were invited to a British temperance meeting, and Wells had the aforementioned quotes from Willard reprinted in a British newspaper. Wells wrote in her commentary that Willard had "unhesitatingly slandered the entire Negro race in order to gain favor with those [in the South] who were hanging, shooting, and burning Negroes alive." Willard concluded by calling Wells a "bright young colored woman, whose zeal for her race has...clouded her perception as to who were her friends and well-wishers."

CHAPTER 9

IN THE CLEAR

TEQUILA, VODKA AND GIN

Sippin' on gin and juice, laid back
With my mind on my money and my money on my mind
—Snoop Dogg, 1993

Every year since 1970, vodka has been the best-selling spirit by volume in the United States. In 2024, the list of best-selling spirits read: (1) vodka, (2) premixed cocktails called ready-to-drink (RTD) cocktails, (3) agave spirits and (4) American whiskey.

AGAVE SPIRITS: DeLEON DISTRIBUTOR DILEMMA

For the last two years, tequila and mezcal have continued to increase their volume sales and popularity. It seems everyone has that story from college, or when they were younger, involving some bad tequila coupled with a night gone wrong. For me, the tequila was Pepe Lopez "Jism" (the nickname in quotes was provided by a fraternity brother). Many a shot was downed, and we bit into a lemon or lime wedge for relief from the burn. Now, craft tequilas are meant to be sipped and savored—and they even have the reputation of being the one liquor that doesn't cause hangovers. Perhaps Diddy had it right when he said of his DeLeon tequila: "I want to touch everybody with some smoothness, so that when you drink tequila, you don't make that ugly face."

On April 2, 2020, the Alcohol and Tobacco Tax and Trade Bureau (TTB) finalized the creation of a new class within its standards of identity called agave spirits. Within this class, there are two types: tequila and mezcal. According to TTB, the standard

> *would include spirits distilled from a fermented mash, which at least 51 percent is derived from plant species in the genus Agave and up to 49 percent derived from sugar. Agave Spirits must be distilled at less than 95 percent alcohol by volume and bottled at or above 40 percent alcohol by volume.*

Because tequila and mezcal are recognized as distinctive products of Mexico, they must be manufactured in Mexico in accordance with the laws and regulations of Mexico governing their manufacture.

In 2013, after an excellent five-year run of making Cîroc a power player in the vodka game, Diageo and Sean Combs (variously known as Puffy, Puff, Puff Daddy, P. Diddy, Diddy, Love, Brother Love and the Diddler—but for our purposes, we'll stick with Diddy) co-purchased the brand DeLeon Tequila from a California company called Quench Enterprise. As described by Diddy: "With Cîroc, we dated. Now, with DeLeon, we're married. This deal is way better. This makes me a true owner." As Larry Schwartz, president of Diageo North America, put it, "Ultra-premium and above tequila is a very exciting segment—we already have a strong brand with Don Julio and are pleased to complement that offering with DeLeon." Part of the calculation was likely that Diageo needed to fill the hole left when it and the brand Jose Cuervo parted ways in 2012.

Following the Cîroc playbook, Diddy didn't waste any time. He threw glitzy parties: at one, in Manhattan, the guest list included Swizz Beatz and Naomi Campbell and had giant *D* logos projected on brick walls. Acrobats twirled through the air above the heads of the crowd. His goal was clear: to take down the current king of tequila, Patrón—or, as Diddy called it, "Mr. Pat Ron."

Prior to the acquisition by Diddy and Diageo, DeLeon was an up-and-coming luxury brand. But it got hooked up with a bad distributor and took years to extricate itself from the relationship. The opinion in the case *Quench LLC v. Liquor Grp. Wholesale, Inc.* from the Middle District of Florida tells the sordid tale of what happened. Things were off from the very beginning. The distribution agreement was signed in December 2009, and the distributor (the Liquor Group) failed to make or severely delayed deliveries of DeLeon to "key prestigious and highly valued clients" in the first two weeks. The distributor also filed numerous depletion reports containing information that was found to be intentionally altered after the fact—that is, when they filed reports at all. Then there was the fact that the distributor failed to pay DeLeon in a timely manner on numerous occasions for the products it had sold. And finally, it was proved that the distributor sold some DeLeon in Michigan, a state it was expressly prohibited from selling in per the agreement. Once the agreement was terminated, it was also shown that the distributor went on using DeLeon's intellectual property by continuing to show that the brand was still within its portfolio. After a year of back-and-forth in arbitration, both compensatory and injunctive relief were awarded to DeLeon. The court then finally confirmed the arbitration award, and the white knight in the form of Diageo and Diddy rode in to buy the brand.

VODKA: THE RISE AND FALL OF CÎROC OBAMA (DIDDY DIAGEO DIVORCE)

There are a lot of reasons for vodka being the best-selling spirit in the United States for over fifty years. For the most part, it's affordable and inoffensive, and it's the easiest spirit to produce. As defined by TTB, standard vodka is a neutral spirit that contains no colors or flavors and has at least 40 percent alcohol by volume. Any number of ingredients can act as the base, such as wheat, corn, grapes, potatoes, rice or fruit, to name just a few. I've counted well over twenty brands that are billed as Black-owned, but the story behind how Diddy took a middling French brand to the heights of the vodka market almost overnight and how it all unraveled in a very ugly divorce is the one I want to tell.

The Cîroc brand was launched in 2003 and consists of vodka and flavored vodka offerings. The Robicquet family that founded the brand has been in the alcohol business since the sixteenth century. One of Cîroc's first American brand ambassadors was a National Football League (NFL) player named Earl Little. Apparently, he was a defensive back for the Cleveland Browns (who that season had a record of 5-11). The brand was promoted at nightclubs and other venues in cities such as Miami and Atlanta. This tentative first step into the U.S. market was not going well.

By 2006, the brand, now owned by Diageo (the behemoth British multinational alcoholic beverage company) was having difficulty. It was moving only about forty thousand cases of Cîroc a year when it approached

Diddy to get involved. (I guess Earl wasn't getting it done. He was traded to the Green Bay Packers in 2005 and left football in 2006.) In an interview recalling the moment, Diddy said, "They weren't doing much, and it was struggling….So I decided to take a chance on the brand. We decided if it does well, we can be fifty- fifty partners." In 2007, Diddy's company Combs Wines & Spirits began a business relationship with Diageo for the marketing and promotion of Cîroc.

Things went very well for the partners, starting with a December 2007 campaign in which Diddy announced that Cîroc was the "official vodka of New Year's." He often called himself Cîroc Obama on social media. Indeed, there were scores of "Barack 'Cîroc' Obama Inauguration Celebrations" in early 2009, where drinks like "Cîroc Vodka Obama martinis" were featured. Taking an approach to branding that *Forbes* called "Cîroc-and-Awe," Diddy marshalled an army of DJs, hip-hop artists, models, reality TV stars, actors and influencers to help him evangelize the Cîroc brand. Check out the 2013 song "Cîroc and Simply Lemonade" by Nelly (Cornell Haynes Jr.), Diddy was a ruthless promoter. Cîroc made countless appearances in his music videos and was mentioned on his Twitter account hundreds of times. From 2007 to 2009, Diddy threw his epic "White Parties," and it seems that at these parties, he and his Cîroc were inseparable. A September 29, 2024 *New York Times* article titled "Sean Combs's White Parties Were Edgy, A-List Affairs. Were They More?" provided this description of one of the 2009 parties:

> *At the center of it all was Mr. Combs, the billionaire hip-hop mogul… invariably toasting the scene with a glass of Cîroc vodka and welcoming comparisons of his revels to those of lore.*
>
> *"Have I read 'The Great Gatsby'?" Mr. Combs once told* [a newspaper]. *"I am the Great Gatsby!"*

In 2007, the brand sold 98,000 cases, and by 2010, the case count was up to 795,000. At its peak, in 2014 and 2015, Cîroc was selling 2.6 million cases.

That army of influencers got Diddy and Diageo into trouble more than once. In October 2011, a video of Diddy himself went viral. In the video, Diddy "was seen cursing and throwing ice at a Grey Goose–drinking club-goer at a packed nightclub, angry that the partier wasn't drinking his brand, Cîroc." In 2017, the Federal Trade Commission (FTC), acting on a deceptive marketing complaint compiled by the watchdog group Truth in Advertising, sent Diddy and forty-five members of his army a letter reminding them of the legal requirements to properly disclose sponsorship. According to the FTC's Endorsement Guide:

> *If there's a connection between an endorser and the marketer that a significant minority of consumers wouldn't expect and it would affect how they evaluate the endorsement, that connection should be disclosed clearly and conspicuously. For example, if an ad features an endorser who is a relative or employee of the marketer, the ad is misleading unless the connection is made clear. The same is true if the endorser has been paid or given something of value to tout the product. The reason is obvious: knowing about the connection is important information for anyone evaluating the endorsement.*

According to TINA, "It is the responsibility of the marketer and the brand to advise influencers of their disclosure responsibilities and monitor their endorsements to ensure appropriate disclosures are made." The watchdog compiled over 1,700 Instagram posts from fifty different Cîroc influencers who had failed to reveal their material connection to the alcohol brand in a clear and conspicuous manner; more than one-third of the posts came from Diddy himself.

The fix for space-cramped platforms like Instagram, according to the FTC, was to start the post with "AD" or "#ad." A 2019 update from TINA reported:

> *Within a week of being notified of TINA.org's finding, Diddy removed all of the Cîroc ads on his Instagram page that TINA.org collected. As of Jan. 7, nearly 90 percent of the posts in TINA.org's entire database of more than 1,700 Instagram ads published by Cîroc influencers, including Diddy, have been taken down. Meanwhile, 180 have been edited, 140 of which to appropriately include #ad on the first line of the post.*

Diddy and Diageo can still be found on TINA's "Wall of Shame."

In 2014, Diageo acquired the Don Julio tequila brand and committed $400 million to grow it. It was at this point that storm clouds began to collect over the Diddy/Diageo relationship. In 2017, the company acquired the Casamigos brand, started by George Clooney and his buddies. In May 2023, Diddy publicly accused Diagio of "racially typecasting" his brands Cîroc and DeLeon. He filed a lawsuit in which he claimed Diageo and its executives "put their feet on the neck of Mr. Combs' brands. In a business where production, distribution and sales are the pillars of success, Cîroc and DeLeon have been starved of resources of all three." The complaint accused Diageo of failing to support Diddy's brands and of marginalizing their appeal by marketing them as "Black brands." It continued:

> *Rather than equal treatment, Diageo has treated Mr. Combs and his brands worse than others because he is Black. Diageo had typecast Cîroc and DeLeon, apparently deciding they are Black Brands that should be targeted only to "urban" consumers.*

In July 2023, the court unsealed documents in the case, and a previously sealed version of the complaint was revealed to read:

> *Diageo showed up in person to Mr. Combs and his team with a developed watermelon-flavored DeLeon Tequila. They did this despite DeLeon not having flavored tequila, Mr. Combs' consistent objection to adding flavors, and the efforts to educate Diageo about the racial history and connotations relating to watermelon.*

About this allegation, Diageo made the point that Cîroc had previously released a Summer Watermelon Cîroc vodka that apparently didn't bother Diddy, stating that Diddy "supported, publicly endorsed for several years, and benefited financially from the success of Cîroc Summer Watermelon."

The complaint alleged that Diageo invested in and expanded other brands (Don Julio and Casamigos) while Combs's brands were left to "wither." It noted that the DeLeon brand was currently sold in less than 4 percent of possible outlets, compared with more than a third for Casamigos and Don Julio tequilas. Diddy intended to "seek billions of dollars in damages due to Diageo's neglect and breaches." The complaint continued, "Cloaking itself in the language of diversity and equality is good for Diageo's business, but it is a lie. While Diageo may conspicuously include images of its Black partners in advertising materials and press releases, its words only provide an illusion of inclusion."

Diageo wasn't having it. The company countersued Diddy in June 2023 and terminated its relationship with him. In one of its filings, Diageo fired back:

> *We are saddened that Mr. Combs has chosen to recast a business dispute as anything other than that and chosen to damage a productive and valued partnership. Mr. Combs' bad-faith actions have clearly breached his*

contracts and left us no choice but to move to dismiss his baseless complaint and end our business relationship. Mr. Combs has repeatedly undermined our partnership and threatened to defame Diageo if we did not meet his unreasonable financial demands. Diageo believes strongly in the Cîroc and DeLeon brands and remain committed to their success, which is why we tried for years to salvage the broken relationship with Mr. Combs. We funded the purchase of DeLeon for the joint venture and proceeded to invest more than $100 million to grow the brand. Despite having made nearly a billion dollars over the course of our 15-year relationship, Mr. Combs contributed a total of $1,000 and refused to honor his commitments.

Diageo wasn't quite done with Diddy yet. The countersuit continued:

In May 2021, following Diageo's public commitment of US $100m to help with Covid recovery for the hospitality sector and under privileged communities, Mr. Combs demanded that Diageo pay him US $100m and threatened to "reach out to every news outlet" to burn the house down and cause maximum damage to Diageo and the DeLeon brand, by making public accusations [of] *racism if Diageo refused to write the check.*

At bottom, [his] *baseless allegations are nothing more than a poorly veiled attempt to weaponize public accusations of racism in order to line Mr. Combs' pockets even further.*

In accusing Diddy of a lack of commitment to Diageo's diversity and equity agenda, the countersuit asserted:

When invited to join Diageo's diversity initiatives, including the Pronghorn initiative and providing financial support for Historically Black Colleges and Universities, Mr. Combs declined to participate, and in fact tried to discourage Diageo from working with other African American business people or influencers on the Pronghorn initiative.

By January 2024, both sides, probably tired of airing their dirty laundry in public, issued a joint statement:

Sean Combs and Diageo have now agreed to resolve all disputes between them. Mr. Combs has withdrawn all of his allegations about Diageo and will voluntarily dismiss his lawsuit against Diageo with prejudice.

> *Diageo and Mr. Combs have no ongoing business relationship, either with respect to Cîroc vodka or DeLeon tequila, which Diageo now solely owns.*

With that, the divorce was complete. According to a Diageo investors' report, Diddy did receive a $200 million parting gift from the purchase of his 50 percent of the share capital of DeLeon by Diageo. After reporting that Cîroc brand sales fell by 26 percent for the year ending June 30, 2024, Diageo announced that it was exchanging its brand rights to Cîroc in North America for a majority ownership stake of Lobos 1707, the tequila brand backed by LeBron James. Out with Diddy and in with King James!

GIN: BLACK COCK VIGOR GIN AND WHO KILLED MARGARET LEAR?

The year was 1905, and the trade card of a certain product told the story:

> *Black Cock Vigor Gin, always all right,*
> *Loads you with courage daytime or night,*
> *A drink that makes men feel good all through,*
> *Cures kidney weakness, other things too,*
> *Kind of puts life in the old and new,*
> *Considered by all great in its line,*
> *Oysters can equal this stimulant fine,*
> *Cures laziness, makes your limbs grow,*
> *Keeps muscles hard from head to toe.*
> *Vigor and vim it imparts and maintains,*
> *Gets up the steam in the sinews and veins,*
> *It gives you the courage to go in and win,*
> *Nothing can equal Black Cock Vigor Gin.*

The double entendres abound in this rhyme as the gin was advertised almost exclusively to poor Black folks in the South. In the May 16, 1908 issue of *Collier's*, the journalist Will Irwin asked the question, "Who killed Margaret Lear?" He recounted the story of a fourteen-year-old girl walking home from Shreveport High School in March 1905. She was on her way home, which took her past a "Negro saloon" on the edge of town.

Black Cock Vigor Gin trading card. *From* Those Pre-Pro Whiskey Men! *blog, November 29, 2018. Photo restoration by Jason Hamacher.*

> *Out of that saloon staggered a negro named Coleman—"drunken," ran the testimony at trial, "on cheap gin." He followed her to a ditch on the edge of a field, assaulted her, and shot her. Margaret Lear, when he had gone, dragged herself along the field to her mother's gate, and there clutching the pickets, she died.*

Coleman was arrested, and even before he got to jail, a White mob had gathered to welcome him. The governor of Louisiana, "anxious to save the name of the state," called out many companies of the state's militia to keep the peace. During the nine days of martial law, the state tried Coleman, found him guilty and legally executed him. Journalist Will Irwin wrote:

> *It is one thing to theorize, it is another to live through such an outrage in your own community. You and I might not have been in that mob which howled for the blood of this poor beast, Coleman, but you and I can not greatly blame the man who was in it. And yet, who was the real murderer of Maragaret Lear? What if he wears a white face instead of black—would you grease the rope for him?*

In his article, Irwin highlighted two brands of gin that targeted "'low negro dives' in the Black Belt that had obscene titles, obscene labels [that] advertised by suggestion, by double meanings that the compounds contain a drug to stimulate the low passions which have made the race problem such a dreadful thing in the south." Irwin identified Lee Levy & Company of 206 Market Street in St. Louis as the worst offender, writing that if he gave the name of the product (Black Cock Vigor Gin) or attempted to describe its label (a scantily clad White woman), his publication (*Collier's*) "would not go through the mails." Irwin also identified the Dreyfuss, Weil & Company product Devil's Island Endurance Gin as one of the products he could actually mention by name, because "they were more clever and restrained in their work." Irwin recalled:

> *In a negro street of New Orleans I saw five saloon shop-windows in one block which displayed either Lee Levy's or Dreyfuss, Weil & Company's. This latter firm is more clever in its work than the others, much more delicate and subtle in its labeling policy. It takes one who understands the negro and his slang to appreciate the enigma of their wording; it all comes in a "caution label" on the obverse of the bottles.*

However, one of the trade cards used by representatives who sold the product contained a picture of a women's beach dressing room with a woman in a bathing suit saying, "Those fellows who drink that Devil's Island Endurance Gin seem to have the very 'devil' in them." The gin was so popular in the Black community that it had a song written about it by Roosevelt "Honeydripper" Sykes in the 1920s—making it likely one of the first specifically name-dropped brands of alcoholic products to appear in a song by a Black artist. Here are a few lyrics from his "Devil's Island Gin Blues":

> *Give me one more drink*
> *Of that Devil's Island Gin*
> *Give me one more drink*
> *Of that Devil's Island Gin*
> *I've been drunk once tonight*
> *And I want to get drunk again*
> *Take me back, baby*
> *Lord, I won't get drunk no mo'*
> *You just take me back, baby*
> *I won't get drunk no mo'*
> *I'll guarantee I'll let all whiskey, go*

For a poignant contemporary description of a "Negro dive bar," here is an excerpt of a *Times-Democrat* article titled "Evil Brands of Gin Sold in New Orleans" from June 29, 1908:

> *If you were to see the habitat of this cheap gin and still cheaper whisky, take a stroll down Decatur Street in the vicinity of the French Market: peer into the foul-smelling groggeries which stud the street and send their nauseous odors into the open.... The floor is grimy, the counter is dripping with the foam of beer and the lees of whisky and gin. Behind the bar are several rows of dingy-looking bottles containing various liquids. Seated at tables, on boxes and on barrels are greasy, bleary-eyed negroes, all in a more or less befuddled state. On the walls are pictures—highly colored lithographs of white women in low neck and short sleeve dresses.*

Irwin's *Collier's* article concluded:

> *Is it plain now—the secret of many and many a lynching and burning in the South? The primitive Negro field hand, a web of strong sudden impulse, good and bad, comes to town or settlement on Saturday afternoon and pays his fifty cents for a pint of Mr. Levy's gin. He absorbs not only its toxic heat, but absorbs also the suggestion subtly conveyed that it contains aphrodisiacs. He sits in the road or in the alley at the height of debauch, looking at the obscene picture of a white woman on the label, drinking in the invitation it carries. And then comes—opportunity. There follows the rope or the stake.*
>
> *And neither the black brute dying in agony, nor these whites, temporary brutes in their mob anger, can see this vision: A gentleman of St. Louis taking his fat after dinner ease, sitting on a plush, decked with diamonds, lulled by a black cigar, and planning how he shall advance his business... to chastise abuses in the retail liquor traffic.*

Dr. Charles Crowe, writing in the *Journal of Negro History* in 1968, described Irwin's conclusion this way:

> *The anti-vice and prohibition causes found a common enemy in the "dives" where Negroes commonly drank cheap gin from bottles with images of "nude" white women on them. Thus the "primitive" black with his "strong, sudden impulses" absorbed both the "toxic heat" and the "suggestion of aphrodisiacs" in the bottle. With every drink the*

Negro stared at the "obscene" label "drinking in the invitation" to the act of "assault."

The effects of Irwin's article were swift for Levy and some of his sales agents. A federal grand jury issued indictments for violations of postal laws against the company for sending obscene materials through the mail. All those initially indicted were found guilty and subjected to large fines.

An editorial on the subject in the June 19, 1908 edition of the *Columbia Herald* reads:

TO THE MANHOOD OF TENNESSEE

What say you to house-cleaning? Or will you wait until some Tennessee family is called upon to furnish a Margaret Lear?…That the liquor dealers of Tennessee at this very time are selling to negroes, Lee Levy & Co's gin with the indescribable label. They are selling it in Memphis. They are selling it in Nashville. The negro comes from centuries of savagery and a century and more of bondage. Liquor fires his savage instincts and brings them to the surface. That he is morally weak is no more natural under the circumstances. He falls easy prey to temptation. The effect of the saloon upon the negro is disastrous to his industry and good citizenship.

Puck was a weekly magazine that featured colorful cartoons, caricatures and political satire of contemporary issues. On this January 16, 1907 front cover, it took aim at the Woman's Christian Temperance Union, one of the organizations behind the push to close dives or canteens, depicting an intoxicated Black soldier shooting handguns in the street while his friend is being thrown out into street from the Red Eye Hotel. The caption reads, "One result of abolishing the canteen, respectfully submitted for the consideration of the W.C.T.U."

Puck magazine front cover: L.M. Glackens, "One Result of Abolishing the Canteen," January 16, 1907. *Library of Congress.*

GIN AND THE DREYFUS AFFAIR

Though "Devil's Island Endurance Gin" had its obvious double meaning, it also had an interesting origin story that bears telling. If you saw the 2019 movie *An Officer and a Spy* by Roman Polanski, you already know part of the story. According to the February 15, 1905 edition of the *Paducah Sun*, the senior member of the local firm Dreyfuss, Weil & Co., one Mr. Sol Dreyfuss, was visiting his childhood home in the Alsace-Lorraine region of France and was hanging out with his brother who still lived there. This brother just happened to be a "renowned chemist and 'distillaleur' of French cordials and liqueors" who shared with Sol the recipe of a promising gin that he thought might sell well in the United States. As for the name of the gin:

> *The name selected for it, "Devil's Island Endurance Gin," was selected by Mr. Sol Dreyfuss and submitted first to Capt. Dreyfus in Paris by his brother in Europe, who made a special trip to Paris to confer with the "captain" and get his consent to use this name, and the design showing Capt. Dreyfuss in the cage on Devil's Island, with the words, "Hope, Energy, Fortitude, Strength, Endurance," all around him in the cage, and the "devils" on all sides picking at him constantly.*
>
> *Mr. Dreyfuss explains his reasons for selecting the name, first owing to the agitation of the famous "Dreyfus affaire" at that time, secondly, the ingredients as compounded in this Gin stand for everything Capt. Dreyfus stood for, "Energy, Fortitude, Strength, Endurance," and all, a pleasant word for everybody.*

Devil's Island Endurance Gin advertisement, November 2, 1915. *From the* Birmingham Age Herald.

In 1894, Captain Alfred Dreyfus was a thirty-five-year-old Alsatian French artillery officer of Jewish descent. He was convicted of treason for communicating French military secrets to the German embassy in Paris and was sentenced to life imprisonment. He was sent to the penal colony on Devil's Island in French Guiana and spent five years imprisoned there in very harsh conditions. While he was serving his time on the island, in 1896, back in France, new evidence came to light that the true leaker of military secrets was a French army major named Ferdinand Walsin Esterhazy. The new evidence was suppressed by high-ranking military officers, and Major Esterhazy was acquitted of all charges after only two days. Dreyfus was brought back to Paris in 1899 and retried. During this time, an intense political and judicial struggle ensued that divided French society. On one side, there were the pro-Republican, anticlerical Dreyfusards who supported Dreyfus. On the other side were the pro-army, mostly Catholic anti-Dreyfusards. Dreyfus was convicted again and, this time, sentenced to ten years, but he was pardoned and released on October 15, 1894. He was fully exonerated in July 1906, was reinstated into the French army and served during World War I, ending his service having attained the rank of lieutenant colonel.

The article about the gin mentioned that Captain Dreyfus gave his consent but

> *modestly and politely declined to affix his signature and written testimonial as to the true scene depicted on the label (which was shown him), for no other reason but for the fact that he had given a solemn pledge a few days before not to lend his signature to anything pertaining to his trial and sufferings on Devil's Island.*
>
> *Mr. Dreyfuss (of Alsace) told his brother to say to his American friends that they do not have to be sick or ailing to any extent to drink this Gin; while it will benefit the sick, it will do this also for those who are well. On this account, Mr. Dreyfuss adopted the motto, "Sick or Well, It Will Tell."*

By its third year of production, Devil's Island Endurance Gin had sold 7,619,410 bottles and was widely advertised as the "most widely sold brand in the South."

"GIGANTIC JEWISH LIQUOR TRUST" AND THE NIGGER GIN ACQUITTAL

That 1908 *Collier's* article by Irwin also had another effect. Somehow, it caught the attention of Henry Ford—yes, the car guy. Henry had a newspaper called the *Dearborn Independent* that he often ghostwrote articles in, and in early 1922, he wrote a doozy of an article titled "Gigantic Jewish Liquor Trust and Its Career." In this article, Henry referred to "nigger gin" as the "product of Jewish poisoned liquor factories" and basically implied that the Jews were responsible for the lawless actions of Blacks. But Henry took it a very anti-Semitic step further:

> *In the South the terrible lynching period came and divided the country into pro-lynching and pro-negro parties, but still no one saw the reason for it all. The race question rose to threatening proportions, Americans of North and South looked at each other askance, there was cooling of sympathy between the two regions. The Northerns were inclined to look at the Southerners as unjust and inhuman in their treatment of the negro, and Southerners were inclined to look upon the Northerners as temperamentally unsympathetic and stupidly ignorant of what the conditions were.*
>
> *Behind it all were the products of men like Lee Levy and Dreyfuss, Weil & Company, to use the names quoted from Collier's.*
>
> *The ancient Jewish policy of Divide-Conquer-Destroy was in operation. Jewish policy favors disunion as a preparation to the kind of union which the Jewish leaders want. Jewish influence was strong for disunion in the Civil War. Jewish influence is directly behind the present attitude of the negro toward the white man—look at the so-called "negro welfare societies" with their hordes of Jewish officials and patrons! Jewish influence in the South today is active in keeping up the memory of the old divisions.*

Henry concluded his crazy diatribe by noting that in enacting Prohibition,

> *The people attacked the only thing they could see—they attacked the stuff and the places that distributed it. They did not see the $200,000,000 Jewish whisky combination, they did not see the sinister devices by which strong drink was made vile and viler with the growth of Jewish control.*
>
> *The people rose and swept away the saloons. They did not sweep away the stocks of liquor. They did not sweep away Jewish control of liquor. They did not sweep away Jewish interest in liquor. They left the source untouched. And that source is still existent.*

A 1912 account from Hattiesburg, Mississippi, provides a look into how an attorney made a unique argument to get his client out of an almost certain conviction. The article "Nigger Gin Gets Acquittal for Accused" recounts how an old Black woman named Amanda Berry was charged with the unlawful retailing of liquor and how the fact that there was a large amount of unopened gin at her establishment when the raid happened led her attorney to this argument:

> *Gentlemen you all know that a nigger loves gin too well to sell it. This can in no sense be considered prima facie evidence of guilt, for it's just like old Mandy said on the stand, "Bos, I got dat gin fo' to drink mahself, and I ain't 'lowd to sell hit to nobody."*

The jury bought the argument, and Mandy walked.

Here is a gem from the June 16, 1915 edition of the *New Ulm Review* in Brown County, Minnesota. I guess they really wanted to crowd to participate in the song "Patrol of the Picaninnies." Actually, the concertmaster specifically asked the newspaper "to publish the words [of the male chorus] for the benefit of those who would enjoy 'singing along.'" Just so I'm clear: *pickaninny* is an offensive term that was used for Black children back in the day.

A Treat For Music Lovers

1. March, "Semper Fidelis" (Trompets)............................Sousa
2. Overture, "La Gazza Ladia"....................................Rossini
3. 2nd Movement from Raff's Symphony "Parting"..................J. Raff
4. Cornet Duet, "Jennie" Polka petite..........................Makoe-Beyer
   Serg. John Watha and Geo. Gag
5. "The Son of the Puszta"....................................Keler-Bela
6. Patrol of the "Picaninnies"....................................Masten
   Male Voice: Sweet ham-bone an possum meat,
   Is the grub for coo ns to eat,
   Good for nigger fat an slim,
   Wash it down wif nigger gin.

15 minutes Intermission.

7. March, "Caesars Triumphal" (Trompets)......................Mitchell
8. Overture, "Peter Schmall"..........................C. M. von Weber
9. Waltz, "On the Beautiful Rhine" ....Keler-Bela
10. Clarinet Duet, "The Swiss Bay".....................arr. by P. de Ville
    Serg. Hy. Kitzberger and Corp. Anton Weiss.
11. A Shriner's Frolic, "The Skibbereen Sheik"........................Tracy
12. "Star Spangled Banner."

"A Treat for Music Lovers" advertisement, June 16, 1915. *From the* New Ulm Review.

CHAPTER 10

DISTILLED SPIRITS

TWO MEN OF FIRSTS FROM THE BIG APPLE

In this country, where a lot of drink culture is owed to Blackness, very little of it is owned by Blackness.
—Jackie Summers, CEO of Jack From Brooklyn

JACKIE SUMMERS'S SOREL: REBIRTH AFTER FAILURE

I met Jackie Summers for the first time on a Zoom call for the BOSS program. He was one of the industry experts brought in to give us BOSS Babies some "real talk" about his experiences and what it takes to succeed in the alcohol game. He told us about his 2010 cancer diagnosis, when he was given a 95 percent chance of dying. He told us about how when he was recovering from the removal of what turned out to be a benign tumor near his spine, he decided to launch his own liquor brand because he wanted to "day drink and be around cool people in the middle of the day in the middle of the week, having good food and booze while making some money." He told us about his Caribbean roots and growing up in Queens, where a type of hibiscus tea dashed with rum known as sorrel was always around. He told us about the trials and tribulations he went through to create a shelf-stable version of the drink: his version contained cinnamon, nutmeg, clove and ginger. He told us about all the red tape he had to wade through in 2012 to become the first Black person in the United States to be granted a distilled spirits plant (DSP) permit from TTB. (Go back and reread that last sentence—2012!) No Black person had been officially permitted by the federal government to legally produce a distilled spirit in the United States until Jackie in 2012.

Jackie told us how he worked to get his Sorel Liqueur to become the second-best-selling liqueur (behind only St. Germain) in the New York City market. He recounted how this fact attracted the notice of a few big industry players who offered to buy him out, how he ended up homeless for a year and a half after all the deals fell through when it became evident that the big industry players wanted his brand but not him and how Hurricane Sandy damaged his Brooklyn distillery space. He told us the tale of how he ran across Fawn Weaver while participating in an industry panel and ended up getting $2 million from a venture fund created by Weaver to relaunch his Sorel brand in 2021.

I had the opportunity to meet Jackie in the flesh at a tasting event in Washington, D.C., in 2023. He was slinging his Sorel, and I was slinging my various whiskeys. I approached him nervously with our best stuff, the Ingleside Terrace Single Barrel #27 Rye, and he graciously tasted it and provided effusive, spot-on tasting notes.

ERIC DOMINIJANNI: FIOR BLENDED SCOTCH WHISKY

While Jackie was busy navigating the hurdles to obtain his DSP, Eric Dominijanni was busy earning the right to be able to include "Major, USMC, Retired" on his future business card for his whiskey brand. I met Eric when our respective booths were serendipitously placed next to each other at the 2024 Black Owned Wined and Spirits Festival (BOWSFest) in Washington, D.C. As I was setting up, I noticed that Eric's promotional materials made much of the fact that his Fior Scotch (*fior* is the Scottish Gaelic word for "true," with the connotations of "pure" and "clean") was the first U.S. veteran–owned and Black-owned scotch brand in the world.

When I met Eric, who hails from Queens with roots in Brooklyn, the first thing we talked about was not our whiskies; we had the age-old talk that veterans from different branches of the military always have once they find out that they've both served overseas tours. We good-naturedly traded war stories (his of Iraq, mine of Afghanistan), specifically about the crap accommodations afforded to the marines compared to what the air force procured for itself overseas. When we finally got around to talking about and tasting our products, I learned that Eric didn't know a thing about scotch before 2014 and that he started down his rabbit hole of learning and blending whiskey after receiving a terrible-tasting "thank you for your service" shot of whiskey from a well-meaning bar patron. I wonder if it might have been Malört? He started by getting a bartender to teach him everything he knew about scotch, and by 2017, he was blending scotches on his own to meet his desired flavor profile. After much trial and error, in early 2023, he released his Fior Blended Scotch Whiskey—which is a small-batch blend of Highland and Speyside scotches.

At BOWSFest, our respective booths were crushed with patrons—so much so that we had to start sharing our supplies of tasting cups before resorting to scavenging cups from other vendors to meet the demand. If that night was any indication, Fior is going to do just fine; they sold out of the bottles they had there quickly. I'm looking forward to seeing what's next for Eric as he expands beyond the few states where Fior is now available.

CHAPTER 11

THE WHITE VIEW ON BLACKS AND THE "LIQUOR PROBLEM" FROM THE LATE 1890s

The Committee of Fifty was composed of businessmen and scholars who sought to investigate all aspects of what they called the "liquor problem." Under the auspices of the committee, three studies were published in the late 1890s: *The Liquor Problem in Its Legislative Aspects*, *Economic Aspects of the Liquor Problem* and *Substitutes for the Saloon*. In the second publication, penned by John Koren under the direction of Professor Henry W. Farnam, there is a section titled "The Relation of the Negroes to the Liquor Problem." In it, we find a fascinating view of what the committee thought were the main issues with Blacks and alcohol from the Civil War up until that time. It starts:

> *No reputable author, so far as known, has seized on the liquor habit to explain the source of the most deplorable social trait observable among present day Negroes—shiftlessness and consequent poverty, the development of a distinctly criminal class and immorality.*

As you can see, we are in for quite the ride. In describing how the investigation was to be conducted, Koren wrote:

> *Interest in the relations of Negroes to the liquor problem has waned perceptibly since slavery day. Formerly, self-interest compelled the masters to check the spread of the liquor habit among them by every known device. The black codes, as is well known, abounded in strict prohibition against the sale of intoxicants to all but white men, under the severest of penalties.*

The Country and City Negro

The subject becomes most easily approachable when the rural and urban populations are considered separately. What applies to the country negro, especially the primitive plantation darky, may not be equally true of his city bred brother, who, if not far beyond him in real advancement, is more learned in the wicked ways of the world.

In the September 16, 1847 edition of the *National Era* (an abolitionist newspaper that was published weekly in Washington, D.C., from 1847 to 1860) there was an article titled "The Law of Slavery in the State of Louisiana (1847)" that gives one a glimpse of the actual text used in a Black Code. For the uninitiated, *Black Code* refers to restrictive laws enacted after the Civil War that aimed to limit the freedom of Blacks and maintain White supremacy.

Law of March 19, 1819

SEC. 99. License to retail spirituous liquors, or to keep a tippling house or other house of public entertainment, secured by bond of five hundred dollars; the condition of which is, that it shall be forfeited, should the principal violate any of the provisions of this act in relation to slaves, or keep a disorderly house or permit an assemblage of more than three slaves not belonging to himself or in his employment.

SEC. 100. No free person of color shall be licensed to retail spirituous liquors or to keep a tippling shop, without giving bond in five hundred dollars, and getting the sanction of the police jury of the parish.

Law of April 2, 1832

SEC. 102. Any trader, pedlar, hawker by land or water, tavern or grog-shop keeper, or any master or owner of any hand employed on flat boat who shall sell, give, under any pretence to the slave of any other person, without written consent of the master of such slave, any spirituous and intoxicating liquors, or make any bargain with such slaves to procure, give under any pretence to such slave any spirituous liquors either by himself or by means of a slave, shall forfeit his license to the State, and forfeit for the first offence not less than two hundred nor more than four hundred dollars, and for the second offence not less than four hundred nor more than eight hundred dollars. Owners or overseers of slaves not subject to this provision.

Thus, Koren choose to focus on the southern rural community of Lowndes County, Alabama—which had its own Black Code—with a population of thirty-two thousand, of which twenty-eight thousand were Black and four thousand White, for his study of the "country Negro."

> *Summing up well-attested facts about the relations of country Negroes, the most striking is the comparative absence of habitual inebriety. They are convivial by nature and delight in the social side of drinking. Abstinence from principle is rare. Once in awhile they get drunk, but rarely go off on prolonged sprees. Steady tippling in the cabins is practically unknown. The effect of a debauch wears off with singular rapidity, and does not seem to weaken them to the extent of incapacitating them for work. Getting drunk is regarded as quite excusable and not particularly degrading. The worst among the women drink freely, but they are seldom seen tipsy. On the other hand, a propensity for liquor does not seem to reduce their earning capacity or prevent employment, as a class they drink much more than they can afford.*

In addressing how Blacks engaged in the sale of liquor, Koren brings up the interesting concept of a "blind tiger":

> *Except as a "bootlegger" or a "walking blind tiger," the country Negro is not likely to engage in liquor selling. He rarely has sufficient capital to buy a license, provided there is an opportunity to get one; and it must be said that the more prosperous show little inclination for this occupation.*

So just what is a "walking blind tiger," anyway? *Blind tiger* is another name for a speakeasy, a place where liquor was sold illegally. It derives its name from the practice of disguising bars as establishments exhibiting some sort of animal display to avoid the lawman. *Blind pig* was a popular term, too. Since Lowndes County went dry in 1890 and had no saloon, Koren described the situation:

> *"Blind tigers," both of the stationary and "walking" varieties, abound. The small country store is the "blind tiger." There is no difficulty getting liquor, but whites procure theirs through blacks, which lessens the risk of white "blind tigers." The Negro monopolizes the "walking blind tiger" business; he carries a whiskey flask and sells drinks at five cents a piece. Some of this retail sale is done by Negroes for whites, but most of it is on the black man's own account.*

A humorous account involving a walking blind tiger is found in the April 19, 1918 edition of the *Sapulpa Herald* in Oklahoma:

> *Eggs Ain't Eggs. Ella Is Jailed*
> *"That ain't no nigger's whiskey; that's white man's licka," were the words of Ella Brown, negress, today when she was questioned in the sheriff's office regarding a basket of "eggs" which she had in her possession.... Upon raising the newspaper with which the "eggs" were covered,* [the police officer] *found two large quarts of Old Hayner goody-goody.*

Ella's story about why she was walking around with the whiskey didn't hold up.

THE CITY-BRED NEGRO

Koren collected his data about to the liquor habits of Blacks living in cities from reports from the following cities: Richmond and Norfolk, Virginia; Raleigh, Durham and Charlotte, North Carolina; Columbia and Charleston, South Carolina; Atlanta and Savannah, Georgia; Montgomery, Alabama; Knoxville, Tennessee; Vicksburg, Mississippi; Lexington, Kentucky; Baton Rouge and New Orleans, Louisiana; and San Antonio, Texas. What he portrayed was not at all kind:

> *Both as to vigor and virtue, Negro life seems to be at a lower ebb in the cities than in the country. In the former, therefore, one must naturally look for a greater degree of intemperance, and relatively to the country districts, one finds it.*
>
> *The frequency of Negro brawls in saloons and their vicinity on Saturday nights makes it seem obvious that the back of all this disorder must be an inordinate amount of drinking; but we should not forget that intoxicants, only in part to their inferior quality, affect the Negro differently than the white man. The former, though by nature an amiable and easy-going being, at an early stage of intoxication becomes impudent, abusive, and quarrelsome. So long as he is tolerated, which is not a great while, he lounges about in the saloon. Once in the street, his hilarity and noisiness continue. When the average white man tries to find his way, the Negro remains at large, and quickly lays himself open to arrest through some disorderly act. Improper conduct on his part is less tolerated than in the white man.*

A majority of the police examined show that proportionately fewer colored persons are arrested for simple intoxication, although a disproportionate number of arrests for drunkenness and disorderly conduct may be marked against them. It is exceedingly rare to find any colored person entered under the rubric "common drunkards."

Much of the too free indulgence in liquors seems to have its origins in the Negro's innate love of show, rather than in a strong desire for drink. With the weekly or monthly wages in his pocket, he dearly loves to court admiration of his fellows by liberally spending, and the bar is a convenient place at which to display his rolls of bills. Treating is everywhere a source of much of the drunkenness. Naturally improvident, and with an ingrained aversion to prolonged hard toil, besides being underpaid, the average city Negro has little to spend for drink.

Regarding ownership of drinking establishments, Koren had this to say:

Few Negroes keep saloons. Thus in Atlanta, Ga., there is only one kept by a Negro; in Raleigh, N.C. none; in San Antonio, Tex., four out of seventy-five in the whole city; in Lexington, Ky., one; and so on. The greatest number of saloons, or rather dives, run by colored men was observed in Richmond. Inability to pay high license fees unquestionably keeps many from becoming liquor-sellers. Neither is the business very lucrative, for the patronage of the dark-skinned proprietor is almost wholly confined to persons of his own hue; and oftener than not these show a decided preference for the white man's saloon, although it usually provides separate bars for the two races. There is, moreover, a rooted objection to granting liquor licenses to Negroes, in as much as this would be equivalent to establishing colored centers of political activity. We are justified, however, in importing lack of inclination for liquor selling among more prosperous Negroes to laudable motives.

Koren's view of alcoholism from the medical perspective is enlightening:

In the medical world, it has long been held that alcoholism or delirium tremens, mortality from alcoholic diseases, and dipsomania occurs less frequently among blacks than whites. Dr. Billings, in his census reports, gives statistics showing the comparatively low death rate from alcoholism among Negroes. Commenting upon them, Mr. Hoffman says: "While it is probable that the Negro indulges in liquor to a considerable extent, there is no doubt that he suffers less in a consequence, and this accounts for the low

> *mortality rate from this cause." He also points out that comparative absence among Negroes of liver diseases is due to inordinate consumption of spirits.*
>
> *Medical records kept during the Civil War indicated that Negro soldiers were much less frequently victims of alcoholic excesses than the whites.*

PHILADELPHIA

Koren choose to highlight Philadelphia as the city in the North to detail the "Negro" drinking situation. In the late 1800s, the city had a total population of over one million, with approximately forty thousand Black residents. In describing the city, Koren wrote:

> *The mass of colored people are servants, laborers, porters, etc.; but with an aristocracy of caterers, professional men and small merchants. A large immigration from the South in the last 15 years has increased crime and poverty. In the Seventh Ward, where the Negroes centre, there are fifty-two saloons, but only two are kept by colored men, though Negroes have access to all.*

In describing a change he noticed in the drink of choice among Blacks, Koren noted:

> *From a habit of excursion, dance, and picnic to a habit of home life, from excessive periodic indulgence to a sparing regular partaking; from a use of strong distilled liquors to a use of beer. This change is distinctly noticeable in Philadelphia. The custom of beer drinking is increasing, but the amount of drunkenness does not correspondingly increase and is perhaps actually decreasing. Excessive use and secret indulgence in liquor is giving place to beer as a table drink or evening beverage, used without concealment of any kind. This change has not gone very far as yet, but it is perceptible, and growing among the great mass of working class Negroes.*

Koren cited extensively the 1897 work *The Philadelphia Negro* by W.E.B. DuBois, the first sociological case study of a Black community in the United States, in which DuBois recounted an attempt to count the number of people who entered certain saloons in the Seventh Ward between eight and ten o'clock on a Saturday night:

> *It is impractical to make this count in all of the saloons simultaneously, or to cover all of the fifty-two liquor-shops, but eight to ten were watched each night until data from twenty-six saloons in the part of the ward chiefly inhabited by colored people were obtained. The results from a rough measurement of the drinking habits of the ward. In the two hours the following count was made for twenty-six saloons. Persons entering the saloons, 3,170. Negroes, 1,586: male 1,372, female 213. Whites, 1,584: male 1,445, female 139. The observers stationed near these saloons saw in all seventy-nine drunken persons, of who a small majority were white.*

Dr. DuBois concluded, "I have not found drunkenness among Negroes ever mentioned as a cause of their losing employment in this city."

Summing up his findings on the country versus the city "Negro," Koren had this to say:

> *On the whole, there are indications that the Northern Negro indulges more regularly in alcoholic drinks, especially those of a lighter kind, than his fellows in the South, but not that he is generally more intemperate.*
>
> *Three important facts are established:*
>
> *1. That few Negroes are habitual drunkards;*
>
> *2. That intemperance is only accountable for a small part of the Negroe's backward condition, his poverty and anti-social conduct, and*
>
> *3. That but in exceptional cases is inebriety a barrier to his steady employment.*
>
> *Evidence of an alarming increase in drunkenness is wholly wanting, but both as to country and city Negroes it is generally observed that the drink habit has the firmest hold on the younger members of the race.*

THE CIRCULAR LETTER

In addition to his analysis of country and city Blacks, Koren, as part of his investigation, sent a series of questions bearing on the "chief characteristics of the Negro with respect to the use and abuse of intoxicants and their effects" to a "carefully chosen number of prominent [White] men from the South of local and national prominence in different walks of life." Each of the southern states were covered and about eighty-five localities reached. Responses to the questions were received from ninety-six men.

Koren remarked how it was interesting to see how far the southern Whites' views agreed with those of colored men.

What follows is a tabulated rendering of the questions and responses:

Questions	**Yes**	**No**
1. Are habitual drunkards proportionally as numerous among the Negroes as among the whites?	13	83
2. Is drunkenness a common vice among Negro women?	10	86
3. Do the Negroes commonly use liquor to excess in their homes or at social gatherings?	19	77
4. Do they habitually buy liquor on credit?	5	91
5. Do you regard the liquor habit as a chief cause of their shiftlessness and consequent impoverished condition?	2	94
6. Or as an important cause?	21	75
7. Do you regard the liquor habit as a chief cause of disorderly and immoral conduct among them?	5	91
8. Or as an important cause?	42	54
9. Is it your experience that the liquor habit seriously impairs the efficacy of the Negro as an employee?	14	82
10. Is intemperance, in your judgment, increasing among the Negroes?	23	70
11. Do you observe that any special efforts are being made to promote sobriety among the Negroes, for instance, by organizing abstinence societies, providing coffee houses or substitutes for the saloon, etc.?	6	90

Koren offered an analysis of the replies:

> *The replies to questions 5,6,7, & 8 must be read with some qualifications. Shiftlessness is by all held to be an inborn Negro trait, for which intemperance is in no way responsible, it is characteristic of the abstemious as well as of the inebriate black, a part of his inheritance. The two affirmative answers to question 5 only indicate that drink is regarded as a chief cause of poverty, not of shiftlessness. So, too, the twenty-three affirmative replies to question 6, which apply extensively to Negroes in populous centres, do not touch on*

the matter of shiftlessness, or "thriftlessness," as some prefer to call it; and the sense of them is that the average Negro would remain poor regardless of his drink habits, but that squandering of a large part of his earnings for liquor makes him still poorer.

CHAPTER 12

COGNAC

BLOODTHIRSTY BLACK MEN AND THE UNOFFICIAL SPIRIT OF BLACK AMERICA

They wanna know who's my role model, it's in a brown bottle
Yo, what's our motherfuckin' motto, nigga? Hennessy
They wanna know who's my role model, it's in a brown bottle
You know our motherfuckin' motto, nigga? Hennessy
Hahaha, y'all niggas can't fuck with this old thug shit, Hennessy
That's what you sippin' on, now what's your name, nigga?
Big ballin' ass nigga named 'Pac
—Tupac Shakur, "Hennessy," 2004

The big four brands of cognac are old—really old. Martell got its start in 1715, Remy Martin in 1724, Hennessy in 1765 and Courvoisier (Napoleon's apparent favorite) in 1809. The story of how Hennessy became 2Pac's favorite beverage is an interesting one. Cognac is a region in France, just north of Bordeaux; the white wine grapes grown on the slopes there are used to make brandy (a spirit distilled from fruit juice, in this case grapes). Back in the sixteenth century, Dutch seafarers sought a less bulky and more stable alternative to wine to carry for their thirsty crewmen. They found that the grapes in cognac were perfect for making brandy. So they imported the stills and equipment and taught the people of Cognac how to distill. Thus, the Dutch name *brandwijn* (literally "burnt wine") eventually became brandy. Taking the wine and distilling it (burning it) made it a more stable product that traveled better than wine.

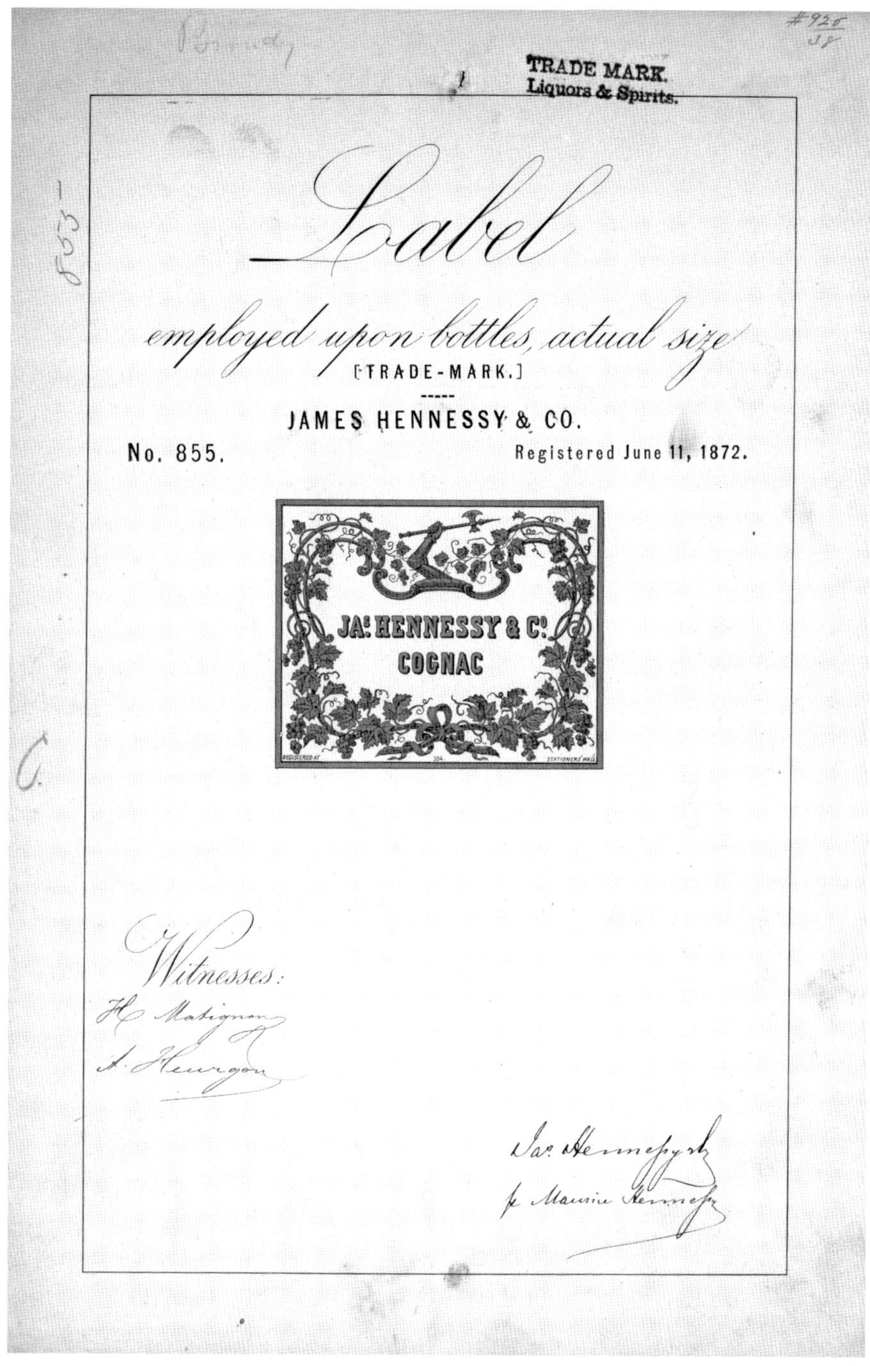

Hennessy trademark, registered June 11, 1872. *Library of Congress.*

The first cognac house was established circa 1643, and from the beginning, one of the primary markets for the liquid was outside of France. Indeed, foreign ownership and investment played key roles in both Martell, started by a British merchant from the Island of Jersey, and Hennessy, started by an Irishman. In 2022, only 2.8 percent of the 212.5 million bottles of cognac produced were sold in France. The other 97.2 percent were destined for the U.S. and Chinese markets. Hennessy was the leading brand in the U.S. market. For close to one hundred years now, Hennessy has been marketing its products to Blacks. As described in the April 3, 2015 issue of *Ebony*:

> *The brand's foresight and willingness to partner and market to the African American community goes as far back as World War I, when Black soldiers stationed overseas first experienced the liquor back at the turn of the century. As the company made its way to American shores in the Roaring Twenties, it was met with the influx of the jazz scene and the budding Black communities on the east coast. The Hennessy family always had a passion for music, so it's a natural fit that the brand would become in sync with the musical evolutions of jazz, blues, and eventually hip-hop.*
>
> *But there was much more than evident synergy in music and culture when it comes to Hennessy and the African American demographic of the early 20th century. One of the company's main partners, the Schieffelin family (a pharmaceutical powerhouse), was particularly committed to investing and assisting in the growth of Black business—one such initiative being the sponsorship of the Tuskegee Institute.*

Let's take an in-depth look at those World War I soldiers and what they faced and just what the Schieffelin connection was. But first, let's set the stage and give you a peek into what the racial attitude was in the United States during this period known as the Progressive Era.

CHARLEY HUGHES'S DARKY TOWN RESORT, 1911

Charley Hughes's (no relation) establishment in the Greenwood District of Tulsa, Oklahoma, must have been quite the place. Greenwood was a vibrant neighborhood of about ten thousand Black residents that was home to several churches, two newspapers and numerous Black-owned business. It was known as the Black Wall Street. At Charley's joint, liquor flowed as dice, craps and poker occupied his customers. Over a ten-year period, there were numerous newspaper accounts of his Black patrons being arrested in police raids. In one, it was said the police "spoiled a hilarious party of drunken gamblers who were holding forth in the place." One such headline from the December 15, 1911 edition of the *Creek County Republican* read, "County Jail Coon Shoot: Nigger Town Scene of Another Bloody Escapade—Was Shot Between Eyes—Nigger's Guns, Whiskey, Craps, Coon Love, Husbands, Etc. Don't Mix in Darkytown." The article describes how thirty-one-year-old Isah Tutt was caught near the Frisco Viaduct the morning after shooting and fatally wounding Anna Beatty. Apparently, Beatty had turned in one of Tutt's friends to the police, and Tutt was none too happy about it. He "worked himself into a fit of insanity which caused him to draw a .38-caliber revolver and shoot point blank three times into the woman." Just ten years later, the Greenwood District would be destroyed during a massacre that was fueled by White fury.

WORLD WAR I AND THE MEN OF BRONZE

The 369th Infantry Regiment of the 93rd Division, formerly the 15th New York National Guard Regiment, landed in Brest, France, in December 1917. Unlike their White counterparts from other New York Guard units, like the 27th, 42nd or 77th Divisions, the Black 15th did not get a parade from the New Yorkers as they left for the front. When the commander of the 15th asked if his men could march with the 42nd Division (nicknamed the Rainbow Division), the answer was no: "Black is not a color of the rainbow."

In 1916, New York Governor Charles S. Whitman authorized the creation of the 15th New York Infantry, which was to be manned by Blacks, overseen by White officers and headquartered in Harlem, where in 1910 approximately sixty thousand Blacks lived. The all-Black unit included a forty-four-piece infantry band that played in France and throughout Europe, led by Lieutenant James Reese Europe. The new music they played, called jazz, caused the French to instantly fall in love. Check out both "The Dancing Deacon" and "On Patrol in No Man's Land" for examples of the sound of the 369th Infantry Band. The regiment began to train under French command due to the need for replacement troops in March 1918. This was supposed to be a temporary arrangement, but somehow, it wasn't, and the members of the 369th never served under U.S. command during the war.

Genuine jazz in the courtyard of a Paris hospital for the American wounded. *Library of Congress.*

In an effort to ensure that the members of the 369th were kept in their place and that the French public didn't treat them with too much "familiarity and indulgence," the U.S. Army issued to the French Military Mission a document titled "Secret Information Concerning Black American Troops," dated August 7, 1918. Its author was one Colonel J.L.A. Linard, and this is what he wanted to convey to the French people:

1. It is important for French officers who have been called upon to exercise command over black American troops, or to live in close contact with them, to have an exact idea of the position occupied by Negroes in the United States. The information set forth in the following communication ought to be given to these officers and it is to their interest to have these matters known and widely disseminated. It will devolve likewise on the French Military Authorities, through the medium of the Civil Authorities, to give information on this subject to the French population residing in the cantonments occupied by American colored troops.

2. The American attitude upon the Negro question may seem a matter for discussion to many French minds. But we French are not in our province if we undertake to discuss what some call "prejudice." American opinion is unanimous on the "color question" and does not admit of any discussion.

The increasing number of Negroes in the United States (about 15,000,000) would create for the white race in the Republic a menace of degeneracy were it not that an impassable gulf has been made between them.

As this danger does not exist for the French race, the French, the French public has become accustomed to treating the Negro with familiarity and indulgence.

This indulgence and this familiarity are matters of grievous concern to the Americans. They consider them an affront to their national policy. They are afraid that contact with the French will inspire in black American aspirations which to them [the Whites] *appear intolerable. It is of the utmost importance that every effort be made to avoid profoundly estranging American opinion.*

Although a citizen of the United States, the black man is regarded by the white American as an inferior being with whom relations of business or service only are possible. The black is constantly being censured for his want of intelligence and discretion, his lack of civic and professional conscience and for his tendency toward undue familiarity.

The vices of the Negro are a constant menace to the American who has to repress them sternly. For instance, the black American troops in France have, by themselves, given rise to as many complaints for attempted rape as all the rest of the army. And yet the [Black American] *soldiers sent us have been the choicest with respect to physique and morals, for the number disqualified at the time of mobilization was enormous.*

CONCLUSION

1. We must prevent the rise of any pronounced degree of intimacy between French officers and black officers. We may be courteous and amiable with these last, but we cannot deal with them on the same place as with the white American officers without deeply wounding the latter. We must not eat with them, must not shake hands or seek to talk or meet with them outside of the requirements of military service.

2. We must not commend too highly the black American troops, particularly in the presence of [White] *Americans. It is all right to recognize their good qualities and their services, but only in moderate terms, strictly in keeping with the truth.*

3. Make a point of keeping the native cantonment population from "spoiling" the Negroes. [White] *Americans become greatly incensed at any public expression of intimacy between white women with black men. They have recently uttered violent protests against a picture in the "vie Parisienne" entitled "The Child of the Desert" which shows a* [White] *woman in a "cabinet particulier" with a Negro. Familiarity on the part of white women with black men is furthermore a source of profound regret to our experienced colonials who see in it an over-weening menace to the prestige of the white race.*

Military authority cannot intervene directly in this question, but it can through the civil authorities exercise some influence on the population.

The French military and politicians pretty much ignored the request of the document to implement Jim Crow, and the Black soldiers serving in France continued to enjoy the "familiarity and indulgence" of the populace, which included discovering the brandy from Cognac.

The soldiers of the 369th were first dubbed the Black Rattlers because their unit insignia included a picture of a rattlesnake. Before long, the French came up with a better name: Hommes de Bronze (Men of Bronze). But the unit is probably best known as the Harlem Hellfighters, the name that their German foes gave them. The unit went on to serve with distinction. They saw combat during the Meuse-Argonne Offensive, which began on September 26, 1918, and as they advanced, capturing towns and key railroad junctions, they lost over 850 men. In recognition of their bravery during that offensive, 171 officers and men received medals, and the entire regiment received the Croix de Guerre (roughly the equivalent of the U.S. Bronze and Silver Star) from France.

THE EVENING WORLD, MONDAY, FEBRUARY 17, 1919.

FOCH TURNED DOWN GERMAN PLEA TO CHANGE ARMISTICE TERMS

COLORED SOLDIERS OF OLD 15TH MARCHING ON FIFTH AVENUE, AND THEIR COMMANDERS

THREE HUNDRED AND SIXTY-NINTH REGIMENT.

MAJOR ESPERANCE. COL. SPENCER.

COL. "BILL" HAYWARD. LIEUT. COL. PICKERING.

GERMAN-AUSTRIA SOCIALIST.

REDS IN RUSSIA URGE U. S. TROOPS TO REVOLT

Pamphlets Call on Men to Demand of Officers They Be Returned Home.

15 WARSHIPS LOST BY FRANCE DURING WAR

PACKING HOUSE WORKERS AWARDED 10 P. C. ADVANCE

GERMANS ACCEPT NEW ARMISTICE TERMS BY ALLIES

GERMAN PAPER KICKS AT WORLD LEAGUE PLAN

FRANCE WILL ACCEPT PEACE LEAGUE RULING

CLEMENCEAU AIDS PLAN TO GIVE WOMEN VOICE IN WORLD LEAGUE

French Premier Also Promises to Support Bill Giving Women Municipal Suffrage.

NEWS OF LEAGUE SENT TO WILSON ABOARD SHIP

Boston Prepares for Reception—To Prevent Suffragists from Making Demonstration.

'HELL FIGHTERS' MARCH ON FIFTH AVENUE AS CROWDS CHEER

SERGT. HENRY JOHNSON IN AUTO, HERO OF PARADE.

CROWD ON HAND EARLY FROM ALL DIRECTIONS.

LABOR PLANNING TO TIE UP WORK IN THREE NATIONS

HE WANTS A PARADE OF THE SUNSET DIVISION

Hammond Asks New Yorkers' Aid in Securing Honors for Westerners Here.

PROTEST IN FRANCE AGAINST BABBLING CRITICS OF AMERICA

Deputy Daumas Says It Is Likely to Alienate Devoted and Trusted Friends.

DIED.

LOST, FOUND AND REWARDS.

"Colored Soldiers of Old 15th Marching Fifth Avenue, and Their Commanders." From the *Evening World*, February 19, 1919. *Library of Congress.*

On their return, the 369th Regiment did finally get their parade. On February 17, 1919, their parade route ran for seven miles (from 23rd Street to 145th Street and Lennox Avenue in Harlem). Both Governor Al Smith and Mayor John Hylan were in the reviewing stand at 60th Street. One newspaper headline proclaimed: "Fifth Avenue Cheers Negro Veterans" and "Throngs Pay Tribute to the Heroic 15th." The *New York Times* described the parade:

> *The negro soldiers were astonished at the hundreds of thousands who turned out to see them and New Yorkers in their turn, were mightily impressed by the magnificent appearance of these fighting men.*
>
> *Swinging up the avenue, keeping a step spring with the swagger of men proud of themselves and their organization, their rows of bayonets gleaming in the sun, dull-painted steel basins on their heads, they made a spectacle that might justify pity for the Germans and explain why the boches gave them the title of "Blutdurstig schwartze manner" or "Bloodthirsty Black Men."*
>
> *Thousands and thousands of rattlesnakes, the emblem of the 369th, each snake coiled, ready to strike, appeared everywhere in buttonholes, in shop windows and on banners carried by the crowd.*

The members of the Harlem Hellfighters were likely the first Black Americans to get a taste of cognac in France. However, there was another American attached to these men who was probably responsible for cognac ensconcing itself in the Black community.

THE SCHIEFFELIN CONNECTION

William Jay Schieffelin was the scion of two powerful families. The Jay in his name possibly comes from John Jay, as he was a direct descendant of the first chief justice of the United States. The Schieffelin family first got started in the pharmaceutical business in 1794. In 1889, at the age of thirty-three, William Jay began work at his family's company laboratory as a chemist. He advocated for the rights and social progress of Blacks throughout his life. He didn't just talk the talk; he also walked the walk. He was the president of the Armstrong Association, named after Civil War General Samuel C. Armstrong, who led the Eighth United States Colored Troops. After the war, Armstrong founded the Hampton Institute in Virginia. The Armstrong Association raised funds for the Hampton Institute and for the Tuskegee Institute in Alabama, which was founded in 1881 by one of Hampton's graduates, one Booker T. Washington. William Jay worked closely with Washington, and by 1896, he was on the board of trustees for both institutions. A January 19, 1905 *New York Times* article indicates that the annual meeting of the Armstrong Association was held at William Jay's house at 5 East Sixty-Sixth Street, where it was announced that one hundred new students had been admitted to Hampton and that the school's curriculum had been increased "to four instead of three years, with a year's post-graduate." William Jay was also an inaugural member of the National Association for the Advancement of Colored People (NAACP), founded in 1909.

In 1906, William Jay hired George Edmond Haines, the first Black man to graduate with a PhD from Columbia's School of Economics. Haines was hired to identify and try to address the appalling working conditions that Blacks faced in factories in New York City (one of them a factory owned by Schieffelin's family) as the executive director of a nonprofit organization established by William Jay. When the leaders of two similar organizations got together with Haines, they formed the Committee for Improving the Industrial Conditions of Negroes in New York City—a mouthful of a name. So in 1911, the organization changed its name to the National Urban League.

Just after the 369th Infantry Regiment triumphantly returned home, William Jay took command of the regiment at the rank of colonel. He replaced Colonel William Hayward, who led the regiment during World War I. William Jay commanded the unit from at least June 1919 until January 1921, when he resigned. As a civilian during the war, William Jay was the treasurer of an organization called the 367th Infantry Welfare League, whose mission was "to keep the line of communication with the home ties that the colored soldiers had left behind." The 367th was another of the Black regiments that fought during the war and included enlistees from New York and Brooklyn. They were nicknamed the Buffaloes. It was during this time that Jay must have heard the first-hand accounts of French libations newly discovered by his men, including cognac. This connection, coupled with William Jay's social activism and what would become his company's new line of business, was likely a driving force behind cognac becoming the unofficial spirit of Black America.

William Jay was the president of the family pharmaceutical company from 1906 to 1923 and then served as its chairman of the board from 1923 to 1929. When Prohibition took hold in the United States in 1920, the company switched from pharmaceuticals to alcohol, albeit at first it was alcohol intended for medicinal purposes. Taking advantage of the loophole in the law that allowed alcohol to be purchased for medicinal purposes, the company became the importer of two of the most prescribed "curatives": Hennessy cognac and Moët & Chandon champagne. One of the likely reasons for the company's abrupt transition, after more than a century in the pharma game, was some bad press that William Jay got from Mayor Hylan, who in a letter to the city health commissioner dated April 15, 1919, expressed the hope that the commissioner would "continue to frighten the druggists who traffic narcotics" and "eventually to get the wholesalers and manufacturers of those drugs." The mayor continued:

> *Schieffelin & Co., the firm which William Jay Schieffelin is senior member…is one of the chief narcotic drug manufacturers and dealers in cocaine, heroin, morphine and opium in New York.*
>
> *While Schieffelin & Co.'s drug concern is manufacturing and selling these dangerous habit-forming drugs for financial gain hundreds of our young men are using such drugs and becoming addicts and committing crimes, some going insane. The police of this city are kept busy apprehending drug addicts who commit crime as a result of its use.*

William Jay filed a lawsuit charging the mayor with libel in response, but his company was soon out of the drug business and into importing alcohol.

In April 1931, as the chairman of the board of trustees for the Tuskegee Institute, William Jay led a group of prominent New Yorkers down to the campus in Alabama to celebrate the school's fiftieth anniversary. At the celebration, it was reported:

> *Daniel Armstrong, son of the founder of Hampton Institute, will present Major Robert R. Morton, head of Tuskegee Institute a medal bearing on one face the profiles of Lincoln, Armstrong, and Booker T. Washington—and inscribed "Hampton Salutes Tuskegee."*
>
> *The reverse side of the medal bears the words of Booker Washington: "I learned that the happiest people are those who do the most for others."*

In 1932, William Jay acted as the chairman of the defense committee for the Scottsboro Boys—the name given to nine Black teenagers who were accused of raping two White women in Alabama. William Schieffelin Claytor (1908–1967), the third Black person to earn a PhD in mathematics in the United States (in 1933, from the University of Pennsylvania), adopted the name Schieffelin out of gratitude for William Jay's commitment to the African American cause. Claytor later went on to mentor Katherine Johnson, the NASA "computer" depicted in the 2016 film *Hidden Figures*.

William Jay had two sons who followed him into the family business: William Jay Schieffelin Jr. (W.J. Jr.) and William Jay Schieffelin III (W.J. III). W.J. Jr. joined the family company in 1914 and was chairman from 1952 to 1962. W.J. III was chairman from 1963 until 1983. After the repeal of

Prohibition in 1933, the company continued to deal in alcoholic beverages as an importer and distributor. Meeting great success, the company shut down its pharmaceutical division in 1962. It is impossible to think (for me, at least) that Hennessy would have become the first corporate sponsor of the NAACP without the involvement of one of the Schieffelins. The same can be said of Hennessy ads being the first spirit advertisements to appear in *Ebony* (1951) and *Jet* (1953).

WORLD WAR II: "LET'S LOOK AT RAPE!"

A series of documents titled "Let's Look at Rape!" was produced by the War Department during World War II and distributed to Black soldiers. These documents illustrated practices soldiers could follow to avoid being accused of rape. One documents instructed soldiers to "beware these women of easy virtue" because they might be tools of the Nazis employed to stir up racial hatred. After all, "Nazis and their fascist friends are not above pulling off tricks like that."

Another, this one signed by "A Negro Chaplain," appealed to the soldiers' knowledge of the growing civil rights movement back in the States. The chaplain noted that rape statistics would be used to continue denying rights to Blacks:

> *There are demagogues who will take rape figures and use them as an argument why those basic American rights for which we have been clamoring*

"Don't drink too much!" From Let's Look at Rape, Record Group 498, Records of Headquarters, European Theatre of Operations, United States Army (World War II) General Correspondence, 1944–46. *National Archives. Photo restoration by Jason Hamacher.*

> *should be denied us. "Look," they will say, "at how the American Negro soldiers raped the women of France. This proves that all Negroes are rapist and criminals. They lack self-control. Shall we turn them loose on the women of America?"*

Based on the admonition from a cartoon that "cognac can get you into very, very bad trouble" and a mini sermon from the anonymous "Negro Chaplain," it's apparent that Black soldiers had developed a taste for the spirit by World War II. Cognac was well on its way to becoming the unofficial drink of Black America, but it took a former sprinting champion to get cognac over the line.

HERBERT "HERB" PAUL DOUGLAS JR.

The next player in the cognac story should have served in World War II but received a deferral from military service to help his recently blinded father run his business. The elder Douglas was later featured in a 1967 edition of *Ebony* as one of the first Blacks to use a Seeing Eye dog. Douglas the younger, born in Pittsburgh in 1922, excelled at football and track. He recalled a chance meeting with his idol Jesse Owens and learning from Owens that at the age of fourteen, Douglas had run faster and jumped farther than Owens at the same age. By 1945, Herb was back home at the University of Pittsburgh. He had previously been at Xavier University in New Orleans, where he was coached by Ralph Metcalfe (who finished second to Owens in the 1936 one-hundred-meter race at the Berlin Olympics). In 1948, Herb made the Olympic team that competed in London. There, he won a bronze medal with a leap of twenty-four feet, nine inches.

Herb finished his degree in physical education at Pitt in 1950 and went to work at his father's garage. Commenting on what came next, Herb said, "More than anything I wanted to be a coach, but Pittsburgh was not employing in the public school system African Americans to be coaches. As a result, I went into corporate. The corporate community was a blessing in disguise." He was hired by Pabst Brewing Company, starting as a sales representative and rising through the ranks to become a district manager.

Circa 1963, Herb was hired by the Schieffelin Company—according to an *Ebony* article, at the suggestion of Maurice Hennessy, which seems odd, given that Maurice Hennessy, the eighth generation of the Hennessy bloodline, was born in 1950, would have been thirteen years old in 1963

Herbert Douglas Jr. *By LBJ Library from Austin. Wikimedia Commons.*

and didn't start to work at the family company until 1975). Herb worked as a special markets manager from 1965 to 1968. He was promoted to vice president of special markets in 1968. As he recalled, at the time, he was only the fifth Black man in the United States to be named VP of a national company. From 1977 to 1980, he worked as a VP of urban market development. He retired from the company in 1987. During his time at the Schieffelin Company, he marketed both Hennessy and Moët to the Black community. Speaking of his time with Schieffelin, Herb said that by ingratiating himself with trendsetters and leaders from the Urban League, the NAACP and the Masonic Order, he was able to increase profits—and that he did. Herb recalled that he was most proud of the fact that when he retired, he left behind three other Black VPs at the company. In 1971, Moët & Chandon merged with Jas Hennessy & Cie., forming Moët-Hennessy. Then, in 1980, Moët-Hennessy acquired Schieffelin. The luxury house Moët Hennessy Louis Vuitton (LVHM) now owns around two-thirds of the Hennessy brand, while Diageo owns the remaining third.

ASTRONOMIC GROWTH OF COGNAC SALES

A look at a 1983 *New York Times* article on Hennessy's announced change in strategy to explicitly target the Black market shows just how much cognac sales have grown in the United States in the last forty years. Hennessy was already the leader in the cognac market (but in third place overall, behind Bacardi rum and Smirnoff vodka, for sales to Blacks). Hennessy's new ad strategy had the goal of increasing sales to over one million cases per year. In 1981, case sales for the top four brands were:

Hennessy:	*615,000*
Courvoisier:	*540,000*
Remy Martin:	*210,000*
Martell:	*175,000*

In 2002, Hennessy spent $2.6 million on thirty-eight magazine ads that targeted Blacks for its Hennessy Very Special Cognac. In 2022, Hennessy sold 4.1 million cases, which accounted for over half the 7.9 million cases of cognac sold in the United States that year. The *New York Times* article described the ad strategy change:

> *Schieffelin's biggest advertising change, however, may grow out of its recognition that blacks are the most important user of this high priced 80 proof spirit. So for the first time a large proportion of Hennessy advertising will be exclusively created with blacks for blacks.*

In 1990, Hennessy was mentioned in the Digital Underground's song, "The Humpty Dance"—the first of over four thousand mentions of Hennessy in rap lyrics:

I'm the new fool in town
And my sound's laid down by the underground
I drink up all the Hennessy ya got on the shelf
So let me introduce myself
My name is Humpty, pronounced with an umpty.

So began cognac's involvement with hip-hop, but unlike with malt liquor, this time around, Black folks got some love by taking some ownership roles in the brands: Jay-Z (Shawn Carter) with his D'Usse in 2012, Ludacris (Chris Bridges) and his Conjure Cognac in 2009, 50 Cent (Curtis Jackson) and his Branson Cognac and Rayshawn Lowe and his Rayon Cognac.

CHAPTER 13

NIGGER WHISKEY AND RECONSTRUCTION

An Inquiry
DEAR EDITOR: I read in a certain paper last week of a boy in your town being drunk on "nigger" whiskey. As it is a new brand, am anxious to know if a fellow can be drunker on "nigger" whiskey than on white man's whiskey and also please tell me where it is made.
—Jefferson County Tribune, *December 6, 1907*

One, here comes the two to the three to four
Tell em' to bring another round, we need plenty more
Two steppin' on the table, she don't need a dance floor
Oh my, good lord
Someone pour me up a double shot of whiskey
They know me and Jack Daniel's got a history
—"A Bar Song (Tipsy)," Shaboozey, 2024

A 1907 newspaper article explained that "nigger whiskey" was

> *made of "neutral spirits," so-called, by keeping it ten days or two-weeks in a charred barrel it assumes the color and appearance of whiskey and is sold as such. The distiller stated that one "can get an ample glass of it for five cents."*

The August 18, 1893 edition of the *Midland Journal* explained the "statistics" of whiskey:

> *A barrel of whiskey at say $2 per gallon which is near about double the cost of the cheap article, called, "nigger whiskey," will cost $.90. A gallon will pan out 120 drinks, which at 10 cents per drink will make $12 per gallon, or $540 per barrel of 45 gallons, leaving a profit of $450 to the barrel. The profit on the cheaper article being greater, as the bummer who lays around the saloons in stormy weather and toasts his shins by the landlord's stove on winter evenings pays the same price per drink as those who get a "nip" at the higher grade article.*

The same question of responsibility was asked about whiskey that was asked about gin, and this 1907 article provides a similar answer, albeit without the overt anti-Semitism:

> *Here we have the explanation of much of the violence and bloodshed wherein the negro is the chief sufferer. Who is responsible? The negro or the white? Do we not, while claiming to be a superior race, tolerate a system that supplies a poison to the negro, converting him into a demon, and then kill him for being a demon? What else are we to expect when we sanction the business that brings the white man and the negro, crazed with potations of neutral spirits from charred barrels and armed with ready guns into conjunction, but the condition described as existing in a number of Southern localities. This "nigger whiskey" is the stuff sold at dives and low dens in this and other cities, and if we are to enjoy immunity from riots, murders, lynchings and criminal assaults, we will have to stop its sale not only to negroes, but to the whites.*

ESSENCE OF OLD VIRGINIA AND THE MINSTREL SHOW

A beautifully preserved bottle label from the Library of Congress shows how a very old importer from New York, A.M. Bininger & Co., took advantage of a popular musical trend that was emerging across the country. The "essences of old Virginia" (also called Virginny) was a slow jig (dance) that became fashionable in the 1850s in minstrel shows. "Dances featuring such jumps and leaps were called 'essences,' the dancer sometimes held his palm…at right angles, while the arms were extended in a sort of pushing gesture." A contemporary press account of the dance referred to it as "a dance characteristic of rude and untutored blacks of the old plantation." For a sense of what the jig might have sounded like, check out Tim Twiss's song "Essence of Old Virginny/Sebastopol Breakdown." A March 15, 1854 advertisement for the "Murphy, West & Peel's Original Campbell Minstrels" show read:

> *They will have the honor of presenting each evening a choice selection of new songs, quartettes and choruses; entirely new dances....Essence of Old Virginia, banjo solos, whistling solos, witticisms, with descriptions of queer, quaint, quiet and quarrelsome darkies.*

Minstrel shows were originally made up of all White performers who wore blackface (burnt cork or theatrical makeup used to portray a caricature of Black people onstage or in entertainment). As one commenter put it, "The purpose of the minstrel show was to show blacks as comical idiots—a variety of clowns.... Blacks in minstrel shows seem happy, and are too dumb to care either way." Frederick Douglass had this to say about White minstrel performers: "[They are] the filthy scum of white society, who have stolen from us a complexion denied to them by nature, in which to make money, and pander to the corrupt taste of their white fellow citizens."

Essence of Old Virginia whiskey label. *Library of Congress.*

A.M. Bininger & Co. ran numerous advertisements in newspapers up and down the East Coast announcing that it imported "Cognac, Sherry, Port, Madeira, 1849 Reserve Bourbon Wheat Whiskey and its own brand of Bininger's Old London Dock Gin." Interestingly, there were lots of ads for the "Essence of Virginia" brand of wheat whiskey in newspapers in Arkansas, Idaho and Washington State well into the late 1870s. From the May 26, 1860 *Weekly Arkansas Gazette*: "Bininger's Wheat Whiskey, 'Essence of Old Virginia' (Put in a variety of forms with a rich label.)"

STAR WHISKEY AND THE SEEDY MAN

In 1865, Democrat Vice President Andrew Johnson became the seventeenth president of the United States when Republican Abraham Lincoln took a bullet to the head at Ford's Theater. When Johnson was a senator representing Tennessee, he was the only sitting senator from a state that had pulled out of the Union who didn't resign his seat when southern states started to secede. He was elected with Lincoln in 1864 when they ran on a unity ticket called the National Unity Party. With the war over, Johnson, as president, pushed for a very lenient version of Reconstruction allowing for a quick restoration of the seceded states to the Union without protections for the newly freed Blacks who were previously slaves. He was at odds with the Republican-controlled Congress, which, on March 13, 1866, overwhelmingly passed the Civil Rights Act of 1866, the first federal legislation to protect the rights of Blacks. Johnson, in his wisdom, vetoed the bill on March 27, and Congress overrode his veto on April 9. Johnson also vetoed bills to provide funding for

"The Freedman's Bureau! An agency to keep the Negro in idleness at the expense of the white man." 1866. *Library of Congress.*

"Distilled and warranted pure by Star Whiskey, C.L. Dixon, Cynthiana, Kentucky." 1859. *Library of Congress.*

the Freedman's Bureau, which was established aid to former slaves through providing food, housing, oversight, education and healthcare and taking other actions. Congress overrode those vetoes as well.

A masterpiece of racial propaganda from the time gives one an idea of the feelings some Whites held about Blacks at the time. This poster, produced in 1866 as one in a series of racist posters attacking the Republicans on the issue of Black suffrage, was issued during the Pennsylvania gubernatorial election. The poster advocates for the election of Hiester Clymer, who ran for governor on a White supremacy platform, supporting President Andrew Johnson's Reconstruction policies. The Black man depicted in the poster wonders, "Whar is de use for me to work as long as dey make dese appropriations?" The Freedmen's Bureau is portrayed as a large, domed building resembling the U.S. Capitol, and its columns and walls are inscribed with what every White man thought every Black man desired: "Candy," "Rum, Gin, Whiskey," "Sugar Plums," "Indolence," "White Women," "Apathy," "White Sugar," "Idleness," "Fish Balls," "Clams," "Stews" and "Pies." At the right is a table giving figures for the funds appropriated by Congress to support the Freedmen's Bureau and information about the inequity of the bounties received by Black and White veterans of the Civil War. In the fall of 1866, the midterm Congressional elections were seen as a face-off over whose version of Reconstruction, Johnson's or the Republicans', would be implemented.

An advertisement for "Star Whiskey" circa 1859 tells quite a colorful story. Unfortunately, I could not find any information about C.L. Dixon or the agent W.B. Crowell Jr. in the sources available to me. Given its tagline, "It Zactly Suits Dis Chile," and the depiction of the minstrel figure on the label, it's not readily apparent just who this whiskey was being marketed to. In the December 3, 1866 edition of the *Burlington Free Press*, a "Star Whiskey" played a prominent role in an article about the Congressional elections of that year. Truthfully, I have no idea if the Star Whiskey in the ad is the same one mentioned in the article (there were a few different Star Whiskeys in various part of the country), but once you read it (that is, if you can make out the dialect), you'll see it seems to fit. If nothing else, it's a humorous look at election integrity.

> *Thirty-Six Stars—Adventures of the Seedy Man—He Tries to Vote*
> *Almost noon to-day, a seedy looking man, considerably shattered by corn juice, staggered into our sanctum, and dropping into a chair, inquired: "Times ed'er in?" We were in: several of us. "Willin' to publish statement from (hic) stranger?"*
>
> *It was raining out of doors, local items were scarce, and we were disposed to listen to the seedy man of shattered appearance—The following was the SEEDY MAN'S STORY.*
>
> *"I 'side in In'nap'—was on An'y Johnson's 'ception c'mittee. When An'y went away he left cons'tution and thir-six bottles of star whiskey in my hands. My heart's full of cons'tution, and my sys'em's ful of (hic) star whiskey. I've been swinging 'round the circle—it's Knights of the Gold'n Circle—ever since. Woke up this mornin' and I thought I was home. Sun'ly 'lected that t'was 'lection day. Havin' gone to bed with boots and hat on, didn't take long to dress. Took gincocktail't breakfast. Started for the polls—little bewildered by gincocktail—run against polls fust thing—one was pole t'n omnibus, t' other was telegraph pole—both 'fused to 'ceive my vote.*
>
> *Shaw hack with sign marked, "Sec'n Ward," got in and taken up polls.—Thought's my ward in na've c'y In'apolis—Called for Dem'cratic ticket, and (hic) d-n man that won't. Saw "Nash'nal Union" on ticket, got mad, tol' em didn't want any Union ticket—want Dem'cratic ticket. Man took me aside and whispered that 'twas Dem'cratic ticket—"Nash'nal Union" only a trick to catch 'publican votes. All right; tried to 'posit—to leave it with the star and (hic) thi'y six Const'ution in the hands of the Judges of 'lection. Asked where I lived—tol' him that I lived right here in In'apolis sixteen years (with 'ception of two years in Can'da during the war) and he ought to know me. Was 'mediately 'rested and led out. Told me ought to go back to In'apolis at once, that I was in Cin'nati—good joke on Cin'nati—being here, thought I would vote a few many times anyhow.*
>
> *Went to Fourteenth Ward next.—Being seedy and (hic) drunk—of which I'm proud—I'ts Dem'cratic—had lo's of Dem'ratic ballots stuffed into my vest (hic) pocket.*
>
> *A vile ab'lit'nis challenged my vote—asked me who I was—tol' him I was 'umble (hi) 'vidual who settled that Ward—had to lay it on (hic).*
>
> *Vote was refused; got on box and spoke—tol' em I'd been drunk with every officer from Alderman to (hic) President—every thing I saw was*

swinging' round the circle—policeman told me to hush up and move on. Asked him if he got a small bottle of cons'tution bitters to leave in my hands—I showed fight—policeman vetoed me over the head with a club—saw thirty-six stars on his coat—knew he'd seen An'y Johnson som'er and it was zall right.

Went to Sixth Ward next; no success there. Policeman said he would take me to the right polls—took me to the Ninth Street Station House. Got out on the plea that I was a political pro(hic)cession. Finally went to Fourth Ward. Fourth Ward all right, took my vote 'thout a word. Goo'fellers in Fourth Ward for cour'cy to stranger from In'aplis. Tol' me to come and vote again after (hic) dinner—guess I'll go 'f I can fin' it. "Rah 'f Johnson."

Exit seedy individual, with the thirty-six bottles star whiskey in his system, and his constitution not greatly improved, although the best he has left in his hands.

The Knights of the Golden Circle, which our seedy man referenced in the beginning of his story, was a paramilitary secret society headquartered in Cincinnati that operated between 1854 and 1863. The goal of the group was to create a new country centered in Havana, Cuba, that was to be known as the Golden Circle, made up of all the states in the southern United States, all of Mexico, all the countries in Central America and the northern countries of South America. Slavery was to be legal in the Golden Circle.

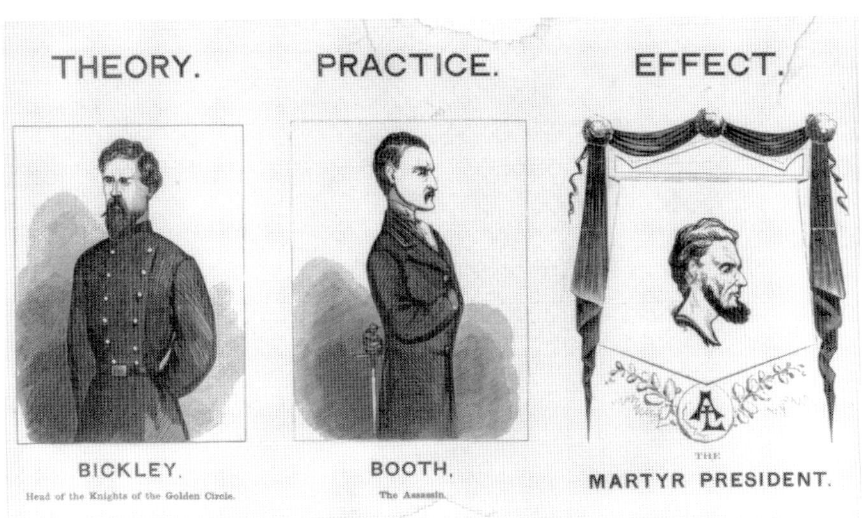

Theory, practice, effect. *Library of Congress.*

A wood engraving attributed John Wilkes Booth's assassination of Abraham Lincoln to the influence of the Knights of the Golden Circle. The portrait to the left is of George W.L. Bickley, "Head of the Knights of the Golden Circle." Above him is the word "theory." In the center, under the word "practice," is John Wilkes Booth in profile, holding a dagger behind his back. The "effect" is the death of President Lincoln, whose profile portrait is framed by swags of black drapery. During the Civil War, Southern sympathizers located in Northern states such as Ohio, Illinois, Indiana and Iowa were accused of belonging to the Knights of the Gold Circle. Despite the seedy man's multiple votes, the Republicans ran away with the election and imposed their version of Reconstruction—and also made Andrew Johnson the first president to be impeached.

CHAPTER 14

THE BLACK BOURBON SOCIETY

In 2017, the spirits industry—especially whiskey—was still marketed almost exclusively to white men. No one in bourbon or American whiskey in general was really marketing to anyone outside this pool beyond a few half-hearted attempts at observing Black History Month and similar occasions. These efforts were both inauthentic and underfunded, making them ineffective at best.

—Fawn Weaver, founder and CEO of Uncle Nearest Premium Whiskey Company

Samara Davis was thinking along the same lines around that time. After falling in love with bourbon during a family trip to New Orleans in 2016, she began experimenting with new bourbon cocktails weekly, sharing them locally and across the country via social media. She also realized

> *that there was very little direct consumer marketing geared towards people of color in the spirits industry. I began to brainstorm how to raise awareness of an emerging trend and demographic of upscale African American professionals who have high disposable incomes, enjoy luxury products and premium spirits. And thus, Black Bourbon Society* [BBS] *was created.*

BBS's website states:

> *BBS bridges the gap between the spirits industry and African American bourbon enthusiasts through social medial platforms, brand-partnered events and exclusive excursions. We challenge traditional direct consumer marketing standards by curating experiences that genuinely engage our*

> *unique demographics and advocate for diversity and inclusion in the spirits industry.*

Samara B. Davis. *Samara Davis.*

Now with over thirty thousand members, BBS has to be the premier Black-oriented bourbon/whiskey group in the United States. I met Samara when I reached out to get her to try a sample of one of our whiskeys (Brown Street Bourbon, I think it was) and to send her a copy of my then just released book, *Whiskey Makers in Washington, D.C.: A Pre-Prohibition History*. In return, she invited me to join the inaugural cohort of the Black Owned Spirits Symposium (BOSS), an invite-only six-month incubator program that nurtures the commercial success of Black-owned spirit brands by connecting the owners with resources to help them succeed in the competitive marketplace. The BOSS program is a part of Diversity Distilled, a nonprofit consulting firm dedicated to advising brands on how to create and implement diversity and inclusion policies within their corporate structures.

BIGGER THAN BOURBON: THE BLUE RUN SPIRITS BOYCOTT

On Friday, July 12, 2024, Samara went live on Instagram to announce that BBS was boycotting Blue Run Spirits and all the brands that are owned by the Molson Coors Beverage Company. BBS had worked and partnered with the Blue Run brand since its founding in 2020. Molson Coors purchased Blue Run in 2023, and in early July 2024 it came to Samara's attention that members of Coors family are the architects of and current major donors to the Heritage Foundation, which created Project 2025 (yes, the same one that President Trump claims to know nothing about). As explained by Samara in a message to her members:

> *BBS is not a political club so we almost never take a specific stand on political issues and while there are certain brands we've refused to work with based on differences in ethics or values, we have not yet publicly*

> *called for a boycott of a brand until now. Project 2025 is honestly a direct assault on civil rights, environmental protections and democracy itself. It will negatively, directly and severely impact all people of color, women, non-Christians and the 99%. It is actively inhumane, and we cannot be aligned with a brand who not only supports it, but whose founders built it and are currently contributing major capital to it. We may not be political but we are and have always been "Bigger than Bourbon."*
>
> *Black Bourbon Society was founded to create space and community and we will speak up when that community is under threat, so we are asking our members to boycott the Molson Coors family of brands to encourage them and other brands to divest from draconian legislative ideas such as Project 2025.*

In 2024, Samara announced that BBS had run its course and would be winding down by the end of the year. Samara announced early in 2025 that she would be attending the Emory University Candler School of Theology. Whatever is next for Samara—and I know that there will be a next—I can't wait to see it!

CHAPTER 15

LANGSTON HUGHES'S JESSE B. SEMPLE ON THE DRINK

Mr. Jesse B. Semple, or Simple for short, was the creation of Langston Hughes (again, no relation) in 1943. Simple was an uneducated Harlem man-about-town who originally appeared in a series of columns in the *Chicago Defender*. From his barstool, he commented wisely and hilariously on many topics. He drank excessively and used the racial situation to justify his actions, such as in *Simple Speaks His Mind* (1950):

Something to Lean On

"A bar is something to lean on," said Simple.

"You lean on bars very often," I remarked.

"I do," said Simple.

"Why?"

"Because everything else I lean on falls down," said Simple, "including my peoples, my wife, and me."

"How do you mean?"

"My people brought me into the world," said Simple, "but they didn't have no money to put me through school. When I were knee-high to a duck I had to go to work."

"That happens to a lot of kids," I said.

"Most particularly colored," said Simple. "And my wife, I couldn't depend on her. When the depression come and I was out of a job, Isabel were no prop to me. I could not lean on her."

"So you started to leaning on bars," I said.

BOOTSIE **By OLLIE HARRINGTON**

'Whoooee, jes, look it him! Brother Bartender, give me some of the same thing he just had

Bootsie by Ollie Harrington, September 26, 1959. *From the* Pittsburgh Courier *Archives.*

"No," said Simple. "I were leaning on bars before I married. I started leaning on bars soon as I got out of short pants."

"Perhaps if you belonged to the church you would have something stronger on which to lean."

"You mean lean on the Lord? Daddy-o, too many folks are leaning on Him now. I believe the Lord helps them that helps themselves—and I am a man who tries to help himself. That is the way white folks got way up where they are in the world—while colored's been leaning on the Lord."

"And you have been leaning on bars."

"What do you think I do all day long?" Simple objected. "From eight in the morning to five at night, I don't not lean on no bar. I work! Ask my boss-man out at the plant. He knows I work. He claims he likes me, too. But that raise he promised me way last winter, have I got it yet? Also that advancement? No! I have not! I see them white boys get advancement while I stay where I am. Black—so I know I ain't due to go but so far. I bet you if I was white I would be somewhere in this world."

"There you go with that old color argument as an excuse again," I said.

"I bet you would not be poor. All the opportunities a white man's got, there ain't no sense in his being poor. He can get any job, anywhere. He can be President. Can I?"

"Do you have the qualifications?"

"Answer my question," said Simple, "and don't ask me another one. Can I be President? Truman can, but can I? Is he any smarter than me?"

"I am not acquainted with Mr. Truman, so I do not know."

"Does he look any smarter?" asked Simple.

"I must admit he does not," I said.

"Then why can't I be President, too? Because I am colored, that's why."

"So you spend your evenings leaning on bars because you cannot be President," I said. "What kind of reason is that?"

"Reason enough," said Simple. "If anybody else in America can be President, I want to be President. The Constitution guarantees us equal rights, but have I got 'em? No. It's fell down on me."

"You figure the Constitution has fallen down on you?"

"I do," said Simple. "Just like it fell down on that poor Negro lynched last month. Did anybody out of that mob go to jail? Not a living soul! But just kidnap some little small white baby and take it across the street, and you will do twenty years. The F.B.I. will spread its dragnet and drag in forty suspections before morning. And, if you are colored, don't be caught selling a half pint of bootleg licker, or writing a few numbers. They will

put you in every jail there is! But Southerners can beat you, burn you, lynch you, and hang you to a tree—and every one of them will go scot-free. Gimme another beer. Tony! I can lean on this bar, but I ain't go another thing in the U.S.A. on which to lean."

CHAPTER 16

A QUICK TRIP UP NORTH

CANADIAN WHISKY

I ran across a picture of a double-fisting beauty at a roadside antique store in southern Maryland. The metal sign likely graced the wall of a liquor store in the mid-1970s. The "V.O." Windsor insisted it was better-tasting than was Seagram's V.O., a competitor Canadian whisky that was released circa 1915. The story behind the "V.O." is that one of the original Seagram sons was getting married, and a whiskey blend was created to celebrate the nuptials; the "V.O." stood for "Very Own." The son thought the blend was so good that he decided to release it commercially. The "V.O." was so important to the family that it chose the initials as its company's symbol on the New York Stock Exchange.

Windsor Canadian, originally launched as Windsor Supreme in 1963, was (and still is), confusingly (to me, at least), distilled at the Alberta Distillers Limited distillery in Calgary. The confusion stems from the fact that Windsor in Ontario is the home of the venerable brand Canadian Club—and its founder Hiram Walker, whom you have to thank if you're a fan of any whiskey with the word *club* in its name (like my very own Mt. Pleasant Club Whiskey). Both V.O. and Windsor are still kicking today. Windsor is now owned by Prestige Beverage Group out of Minnesota (bought from Beam Suntory), and Seagram's V.O. brand is now owned by Sazerac (bought from Diageo).

If recent (2022) sales by volume have anything to say about which whiskey tastes better, it seems that Windsor is currently winning the battle:

Windsor Supreme Canadian Whisky advertising tin. *Jason Hamacher*.

1. *Crown Royal*
2. *Black Velvet*
3. *Canadian Club*
4. *Canadian Mist*
5. *Rich & Rare*
6. *Windsor Supreme Canadian*
7. *Seagram's V.O.*
8. *Canadian LTD*
9. *Pendleton*
10. *Canadian Hunter*

CHAPTER 17

THE COLONIAL PERIOD

RUM AND THE SLAVE TRADE

Molasses to rum to slaves
Tisn't morals, tis money that saves
Shall we dance to the sound
Of the profitable pound
In molasses and rum and slaves
—Sherman Edwards, from the musical 1776,
Tony Award winner for Best Musical in 1969

In 1619, the Virginia Colony enacted a law against the excessive use of alcohol to "strictly regulate drinking." This was also the year the first twenty Blacks landed at Jamestown. These earliest Blacks were considered servants and not slaves at first. This didn't change until a 1661 law was passed that changed their status. A similar Maryland law from 1663 read:

> *All Negroes or other slaves to be hereafter imported into the province shall serve "durante vita," and all children born of any Negro or slave shall be slaves as their fathers were for the term of their lives.*

The Blacks in what would become the United States were to be enslaved and denied the rights of other men. In his seminal book from 1965 on the topic titled *Alcohol and the Negro: Explosive Issues*, John R. Larkins commented on two issues, the control of alcoholic beverages and the legal status of the "Negro":

> *The decisions, laws, practices and policies made concerning these two issues had and continue to have far-reaching influence and impact upon our social, economic, political and religious institutions. From all indications, future generations will have to wrestle with both of these issues, and they will continue to create problems and conflicts.*

As Blacks increased in number and spread throughout the colonies, fears of uprisings and insurrections resulted in Whites enacting a body of laws to control the activities of Blacks, both in the North and the South. Known as slave codes, these laws governed every aspect of a slave's life. They originally existed as a means of convenience for slave owners rather than for security against slave revolts or uprisings and were first enacted in the colony of Maryland in the 1660s and then in the colony of New Jersey in the 1690s. The preamble of one such law declared that Blacks frequently stole from their masters and sold the stolen goods. The purpose of the law was to penalize the White receiver of the goods, in hopes that Blacks would thereby have no one to sell to. To accomplish this goal, persons were prohibited from "buying, selling or trading" with "any Negro slave or Indian slave for any rum, brandy, wine or strong drink or goods, wares or commodities living or dead within this province." The law sought to punish Blacks who "bring or [offer] to sell, barter or trade," any goods without their master's permission. The act also authorized any White person to whip the "wayward Black"; the master had to pay the whipper a fee of half a crown.

A similar 1692 law from neighboring Pennsylvania, "an Act for suppressing selling Rum and etc. to Negroes and Indians," stipulated that a convicted seller had to pay a steep fine of five pounds. In what was possibly a nod to the Quakers' mild view on slavery, the last section of the law indicated that the giving of "strong liquor" for medicinal reasons was not a violation of the act—so it was acceptable to provide a slave or a Native American alcohol for medical reasons. According to O.R. Williams's 1970 doctoral thesis, "Blacks and Colonial Legislation in the Middle Colonies," it wasn't until 1712 that Blacks were considered a threat to public safety. It was the New York Slave Revolt of 1712 in New York City that drove the change. Though the incident did more psychological than material damage, it unleashed a White fear that remained for decades.

THE NEW YORK SLAVE REVOLT OF 1712

Much planning went into the insurrection. Shortly after midnight on April 7, 1712, the house of one Peter Van Tilburgh was set on fire. This was the signal for the insurrection to commence. As the fire spread, dazed and sleepy citizens came to see what was going on. Awaiting the White gawkers were armed Blacks wielding "firearms, some with swords and others with knives and hatchets." As the Whites approached, shots were fired, resulting in the deaths of seven Whites; six others were wounded. The rebel Blacks escaped to the woods, where the roused militia later surrounded them and began to hunt them. Of the twenty-seven Blacks convicted, twenty-one were executed. As Williams recorded, the methods of execution varied according to the horrendous thinking of the court:

> *Some were burnt, others hanged, one broke on the wheel, and one hung alive in chains in the town, so that there has been the most exemplary punishment inflicted that could be possibly thought of, and which only this act of assembly could justify.*

The first slave code of New York came in reaction to the 1712 insurrection. It was titled "An Act for preventing suppressing and punishing the conspiracy and insurrection of Negroes and other slaves" and passed on December 10, 1712. The code reenacted many existing slave regulations, "such as the one forbidding trade with slaves, unless authorized by their master." According to Christine Sismondo in her book *America Walks Into a Tavern*, there were at least ten New York drinking establishments regularly serving slaves in the early eighteenth century. New Jersey, in reaction to the insurrection, also passed its first major slave code, titled "An Act for Regulating of Slaves," on March 11, 1713. This law also reestablished a previous restriction, but this time, it prohibited "any free person from trading or selling rum, wine, beer, cider or other strong drink or any other chattels, goods, wares, or commodities to any Negro, Indian or Mulatto slaves without the master's consent."

Violations carried a penalty of twenty shilling for the first offense and forty shillings for the second and future offenses. Pennsylvania changed its original slave codes of 1700 and 1705 in 1725–26. One section of the new code stated, "Any Negro found in or near a tavern where strong liquors were sold, or found absent from his master with permission after nine o'clock was to be whipped on his or her naked back at his master's expense. Punishment was not to exceed ten lashes."

THE GREAT NEGRO PLOT OF 1741

The winter of 1741 was severe in the city of New York. To the north and west stood the French and Indians, there was a threat of Spanish pirate raids and then there were unruly slaves, who made up one-fifth of the population. Since the 1712 insurrection, slave codes had become more restrictive and stringent to prevent slaves from assembling. But assemble and communicate they did—especially with crews of foreign ships. The fear of Spanish and French invasions and the presence of unruly slaves created a state of mind for the White folks that exaggerated every danger and gave credence to every rumor. England was at war with Spain, and the French were pressing on the frontier.

On March 8, 1741, a suspicious fire burned the official residence of the province's governor to the ground. In the next few weeks, nine more serious fires burned important buildings down. The city's population was in a state of panic, and Judge Daniel Horsmanden of the Supreme Court of Judicature was charged with leading an inquiry into the cause of the fires. A court convened in city hall on April 21, 1741, and a grand jury was empaneled for the investigation.

The star witness at the inquiry was a sixteen-year-old Black indentured servant named Mary Burton. She belonged to John Hughson, a White tavernkeeper, who allegedly ran the establishment, which served as the local meeting place for many Blacks. The name of the infamous tavern was Oswego, and Hughson had been convicted of openly serving Blacks right after it opened but was let off because it was his first offense. According to Christine Sismondo:

> *Oswego went on to become a huge hit among slaves for its Sunday, after-church "great feasts," consisting of mutton, goose, rum, cider, and punch. The place was lively throughout the week, slaves popping in en route to and/or from household errands, and known for dancing, live music, cockfights, and frank discussions about the harsh conditions under which they lived.*

When Mary appeared before the grand jury, she refused to take the oath to testify truthfully. When threatened, she held fast. When Judge Horsmanden promised the full protection of the law, freedom from her indenture and one hundred pounds, she still remained silent. However, when threatened with jail, she relented and offered to testify. She spoke of a plot by a group of people to burn the city to the ground and to murder all its inhabitants. Included in the accused group were Hughson and his wife, Sarah, who were indicted for "conspiring, confederating, and combining with divers negroes and others, to burn the city of New-York, and also to kill and destroy the inhabitants thereof."

In commenting on the lax enforcement of the 1702 slave law that prohibited any trade with slaves, enacted because of establishments that provided liquor to slaves in exchange for stolen goods, Judge Frederick Phillipse, in an address to a grand jury that was empaneled to investigate the incident, stated:

> *I cannot omit recommending to your serious and diligent inquirers to find out and present all such persons who sell rum and other strong liquor to Negroes. It must be obvious to everyone that there are too many of them in this city who under pretense of selling what they call a penny dram to a Negro, will sell him as many quarts or gallons of rum as he can steal money or goods to pay for. This notion of its being lawful to sell a penny dram, a penny-worth to a slave without the consent of his master has prevailed; but this I am sure of, that there is not only no such law, but that the thing of it is directly contrary to an act of the Assembly now in force, for the better regulating of slaves.*

When all was said and done, Mary Burton's testimony and the official court actions of Judge Horsmanden and his fellow judges, James DeLancey and Frederick Phillpse, resulted in the arrest of 154 Blacks (mostly slaves) and 20 Whites. Of those arrested, 31 were executed, 18 hanged (including 4 Whites) and 13 burned at the stake; 70 Blacks were exiled and sold to the West Indies. Hughson was one of the Whites sentenced to death; he was hanged and his body left for New Yorkers to view.

According to historians, much of the testimony that led to those convictions and subsequent death sentences was questionable at best, and no lawyers in New York were willing to represent those accused of the plot, whether Black or White. In condemning the entire episode, historians William Bryant and Sydney Gay, in their 1879 book *A Popular History of the United States*, characterized the proceedings:

> *For its disregard of all rules of legal evidence, for its prostitution of forms of law for the perpetration of cruelty, for popular credulity and cowardice, for the abnegation of all sense of mercy, for the oppression of the weakest and defenceless, it was without precedent, and has had no parallel in any civilized community.*

The New York General Assembly passed a law that heavily fined tavernkeepers who served strong drink to slaves or indentured servants. In New Jersey in 1751, legislation was passed to

> *restrain tavern keepers and others from selling strong liquor to servants, Negroes and Mulatto slaves and to prevent Negroes and Mulatto slaves from meeting in large companies, from running about at night and from hunting or carrying a gun on the Lord's Day.*

Tavern owners had to take an oath declaring that they would not sell strong liquor to slaves without the master's consent. Blacks were also prohibited from meeting in companies of more than five, unless in the service of their master. The law did not prohibit Blacks from attending worship services or funerals. Any Black found to have violated the law received twenty lashes. A 9:00 p.m. curfew was placed on slaves, and any violation of that provision also warranted twenty lashes.

Both the 1712 and the 1741 incidents in New York City created apprehension in the upstate capital, Albany, on the part of slaveholders—mainly due to the fact that most of the slaves there were in domestic service. Throughout the colonial period, the local Albany government struggled with how to keep Whites from providing strong liquor to Blacks:

> *August 1, 1703—Resolved, that the Constables doe take their turns upon the sabbath day to inspect all Tavern Keepers within the Citty, that all Indians and Negroes found in any Tavern as aforesaid, that such Tavern Keeper so found to draw Strong Liquor whatsoever to any Negro or Negroes, Indian or Indians, whatsoever, upon the Sabbath Day as aforesaid, shall pay as a fine for each such Default the summe of 6s, for any such Indian or Indians so found, and for the Negroes according as the acts of Assembly directs.*

By 1768, Albany was trying a different approach: the city sold lots for the purpose of "commerce" to four Albany businessmen with the stipulation that "if any of the above shall keep a bad house or sell liquor to Negroes, upon proof, they shall forfeit their lots." The Tavern-Keepers Act of 1773 was one of the last acts passed by the colonial assembly in Albany that involved Blacks. Titled "An Act for the Better Regulations of Public Inns and Taverns," it prohibited "selling Spiritous Liquor of any kind, to any Apprentice, Servant, or Negro or other Slave." The penalty for a violation rendered the tavernkeeper ineligible to receive any tavern license for three years.

RUM AND JOE FROGGERS COOKIES

"Black Joe" was the name the locals gave the guy who was the namesake of Joe Froggers cookies. His real name was Joseph Brown, and he was born a slave in Rhode Island circa 1750. His mother was Black, and his father was a member of the Wampanoag Tribe of Gay Head on Martha's Vineyard. Joe earned his freedom while fighting in the Revolutionary War. He married Lucretia Thomas Brown in 1793, and they lived in Marblehead, Massachusetts, which at the time was a rough-and-tumble seaport—not the wealthy enclave and yachting center that it is now.

Joe and Lucretia ran the aptly named Joe's Tavern, which was situated on Gingerbread Hill in a building that was also their house. The building still stands and is now a private residence. The integrated place was known for its drinking, gambling and dancing. According to legend, Lucretia developed a cookie there. These big cookies, essentially gingerbread, with spices such as cloves, nutmeg and allspice, were made with molasses and rum. The name Joe Frogger came from Joe's first name and, supposedly, the large frogs found in the nearby body of water, named Black Joe's Pond. Marblehead-based fishermen and sailors took these cookies to sea and they stayed fresh for months: with the rum and molasses base instead of dairy and eggs, they never went stale.

Lucretia outlived Joe by some twenty-two years, and the cookies likely provided a way for her to achieve economic independence; she also sold homemade perfumes distilled from rose petals and baked wedding cakes to help make ends meet. She applied for and received a pension for Joe's service in the war as well. A memorial erected in 1976 provided by the town of Marblehead for Joe reads: "Marblehead's Black Joe, a Revolutionary Soldier & Respected Citizen."

In 1923, some 190 years after Joe's death, Wallace D. Reed published this poem about Joe's exploits:

Old Black Joe lived on Gingerbread Hill,
At the end of Gingerbread Lane,
With his wife, Aunt Crese, he kept good cheer,
And welcomed all comers from far and near,
With 'lection cakes and homemade beer,
And a smile that was never in vain.
He'd tell you tales of the days gone by,
Of the ships that sailed the sea,

Of the pirates bold and the battles fought,
Of the treasures won and the treasures sought,
And the things that were yet to be.
He'd tell you tales of the Indian days,
Of the wigwams in the wood,
Of the braves that roamed the forest wide,
Of the dusky maidens that by their side,
In the moonlight danced and swayed and sighed,
Till the morning light they stood.
He'd tell you tales of the Marblehead boys,
Of the days of the Revolution,
Of the fights they fought and the deeds they did,
Of the blood they shed and the lives they hid,
Of the things they said and the things they forbid,
And the things that were the solution.
So here's to Old Joe and his Gingerbread Hill,
And his tales of the days gone by,
May his shadow never grow less,
May his heart be light and his spirit bless,
May his tales be told with never a mess,
And his memory never die.

Joe Froggers cookies are still a thing: next time you're in Marblehead, take a look, and you will find them. Rum and molasses were integral parts of the Joe Froggers, and rum was the first alcoholic drink in America. In eighteenth-century New England, nothing was more important. Molasses, a byproduct of refining sugar, is the base for rum. By 1770, there were close to one hundred rum distilleries located in the New England colonies, and they made up one-third of the triangular circuit that brought Africans to America.

RUM AND THE SLAVE TRADE

The basic outline goes like this: New England rum distilleries turned molasses into rum, the rum was shipped to Africa and traded for captives (slaves), the slaves were sold in the Caribbean and the ships returned to New England with molasses. From between 1730 to its abolition in 1808, the American rum for slaves trade (not counting the years 1776–83, when the trading took a pause during the Revolutionary War) averaged about twenty voyages a year. As pointed out in Sean Kelley's work "American Rum, African Consumers, and the Transatlantic Slave Trade":

> *Over this period, the peak of the American slave trade, rum accounted for 85–90 percent of the value of all trade goods. In contrast, spirits, including both rum and brandy, made up about two percent of the value of goods carried aboard British vessels.*

Brazilian slavers dealt in cachaça (a liquor distilled from sugarcane) and gerebita (a type of rum) but also traded textiles. Aguardiente (anise-flavored liqueur derived from sugarcane) was traded by Cuban slavers, but they also traded textiles. The Americans traded almost exclusively with rum, with a little tobacco on the side. Kelley provided specific examples:

> *Trade books from the Rhode Island vessels Marygold and Adventure, which sailed in 1759 and 1773, respectively, reveal that their masters used rum to pay 99 percent of the total purchase price of their captives. On the 1770 voyage of the Newport brig Othello, rum accounted for about 94 percent of the purchase price of captives, and in 1803 the master of the Bristol schooner Punch agreed to trade his entire cargo of 6,000 gallons of rum for forty-eight captives.*

So for the trade involving the *Bristol*, a human captive was worth about 125 gallons of rum. For reference, the standard-size barrel used today is 53 gallons.

CHAPTER 18

MALT LIQUOR

AN ODYSSEY OF ADVERTISEMENT IN SIGHT AND SOUND

In a black can,
Why don't you grab a 6-pack
and get your girl in the mood quicker
and get your jimmie thicker
with St. Ides malt liquor
—Ice Cube, St. Ides malt liquor commercial, 1993

First things first: malt liquor contains no liquor whatsoever. It is a variant of beer. "Standard" beers usually have an alcohol by volume (ABV) of between 3.5 and 4 percent. Some dudes in the 1930s in the Midwest (Michigan and Minnesota) figured out how to make a beer with a higher ABV and named the monstrosity malt liquor. No story about this uniquely American version of beer can be properly told without citing the works of two writers: Kihm Winship's article "A Story Without Heroes: The Cautionary Tale of Malt Liquor" and Dave Infante's article "The Sleazy and Spectacular History of Malt Liquor."

No segment in the alcohol industry has ever had better names for its products than the malt liquor category. From Clix to Power Master, the story of malt liquor is a walk through target marketing. From malt liquor's birth in the late 1930s until the mid-1960s, its target market was middle-class White people. According to Winship, this new category of beer, with brand names such as Sparkling Stite and Country Club, "was advertised in magazine ads with neatly dressed, smiling white people, enjoying themselves in festive but polite manner, drinking out of frosty glasses filled from 8-ounce cans."

Trenton, New Jersey's Champale debuted in 1952 and sought to compare itself with champagne. Here is the text of one of its print ads from the 1950s:

> *Champale is like nothing you've ever tasted, except champagne. It even pours like champagne. Pale, bubbly, festive. The kind of thing that goes well with just about any occasion. Or no occasion.*
>
> *But Champale is an alcoholic beverage that costs only pennies more than beer—and you can buy it anywhere beer is sold. So you'll have a hard time deciding when not to drink it.*
>
> *Champale Malt Liquor's bouquet and flavor are at their best when served wee-chilled in a champagne glass.*
>
> *Do that often enough and there may not be any non-occasions left.*

The year 1963 marked the beginning of a change in the marketing of malt liquor. A marketing executive at Baltimore's National Brewing (of National Bohemian a.k.a. Natty Bo fame) named Dawson Farber came up with the name Colt 45 for the company's new malt liquor. He told the graphic designer that he wanted a label with a kicking horse and a horseshoe. No more were they going to hide the potent kick of their product. A year later, the Joseph Schlitz Brewing Company introduced its iconic raging bull. I can still recall seeing that Schlitz Malt Liquor bull busting down walls in the commercials from the 1970s. Turns out that black longhorn Brahman bull was named Zane and was from a farm just outside of Los Angeles. Apparently, he was neutered in his youth and was said to be as gentle as a lamb. But in one of its first print ads, Schlitz Malt Liquor featured a very White woman named Mildred with some pearls from her necklace between her teeth and the text:

> *Mildred never used to be famous for her parties.*
>
> *Then she introduced Schlitz Malt Liquor. This congenial new drink gets its strength of character from 10 malts and 3 hops. Bold enough to serve "on the rocks." Smooth enough to drink "straight up."*
>
> *Mildred still isn't famous for her parties. But at least nobody leaves early anymore.*

Sometime in the early 1960s beer executives began to notice that Blacks were starting to buy malt liquor with greater frequency. In an effort to capitalize on this fact, they started to target their marketing to Blacks. Maier Brewing out of Los Angeles brought out its Soul Stout Malt Liquor and Soul Mellow Yellow Beer in 1967. Unfortunately for Maier, the releases were too close to the 1965 Watts Riots—six days of civil unrest motivated by anger at the racist and abusive tactics employed by the Los Angeles Police Department—and the beers were met with protests and eventually abandoned.

Champale even got into the act. It ran a number of print ads in the early 1970s showing beautiful young Black people extoling the virtues of Champale. Anheuser-Busch tried jumping on the train as well. In 1973, it introduced its lamely and tamely named product called Budweiser Malt Liquor Limited, with the tagline, "Open up with the soul grabber." The brand never caught on, for some reason. The Commodores appeared in Schlitz's 1979 ad campaign, "Schlitz makes it great." Richard Roundtree, dressed as Shaft, appeared in Schlitz's 1982 campaign, "No one does it like the Bull," with the text, "The Bull and I have come a long way together." In 1984, Anheuser-Busch rebooted its malt liquor, this time under the brand name King Cobra and, in 1985, had the footballer turned Blaxploitation film star Fred Williamson in one of their ads.

The malt liquor game changed again in 1986, when Colt 45 released an ad campaign featuring William December Williams Jr., a.k.a. Billy Dee Williams, fresh off his second appearance as Lando Calrissian in the 1983 film *The Empire Strikes Back*. Billy Dee was a bona fide Black sex symbol. I was thirteen when *Empire* came out, and I know I wanted to be like that dude. The ad showed Williams holding a can of Colt 45, with his tie pulled down a bit and a hot Black woman draped on his shoulder, under the tagline, "It works every time!" Sex had been introduced into the malt liquor landscape. Hornell Brewing Company rolled out its Midnight Dragon Special Reserve Malt Liquor with an ad that featured a woman in red lingerie holding a bottle of the product with a straw in between her lips under the tagline, "I could suck on this all night." When people protested, one of the owners of Hornell was quoted in the *Wall Street Journal* as saying, "Real men like sex, and sex sells beer." Fair enough. The gloves were now off.

A MUSICAL INTERLUDE: A LITTLE HISTORY OF BOOZE IN BLACK MUSIC

Researchers trawling through music lyrics websites have identified close to 150 songs released between 1924 and 2006 that focus on alcohol and other drug intoxication, addiction or recovery in the Black community. They range from (1) songs that catalog alcohol use and its related problems,

(2) songs where alcohol is celebrated and used to socialize and signify status and (3) songs portraying the ritualized use of alcohol "to blunt emotional pain, assuage grief, and ritually honor the passing of loved ones."

In category 1, there are such songs as Ma Rainey's 1924 "Blues and Booze," in which she sings that she "spent every dime on liquor," but she had to "have the booze to go with the blues." Lucille Bogan had a 1934 song called "Drinking Blues," Scrapper Blackwell had his 1935 "Bad Liquor Blues," Ida Cox had her 1928 "Booze Crazy Man Blues" and Joshua White had his 1935 "Pigmeat and Whiskey Blues."

In the 1940s, there was Merline Johnson's 1947 "Bad Whiskey Blues" and Billy Valentine's 1949 "Beer Drinking Baby." The 1950s brought us such wonders as the Clovers and their 1952 "One Mint Julep," which tells the story of a guy who ended up married because of one mint julep. Ray Charles later covered this song in 1961 and hit no. 8 on the charts. Champion Jack Dupress had his 1954 "Drunk Again," and Joe Liggins, the same year, had his "Whiskey, Women and Loaded Dice." Finally, there are the Checkers and their 1954 "I Wasn't Thinkin', I Was Drinkin," which tells the tale of a guy who fathered a baby while drunk and answered the judge in defense of this actions with the name of the song.

In category 2, celebratory songs, we have Floyd Dixon and his 1954 "Hey Bartender" and Granville "Stick" McGhee and his 1949 "Drinkin' Wine Spo-Dee-O-Dee." Jimmy Rogers had his 1972 "Sloppy Drunk," and John Lee Hooker covered "One Bourbon, One Scotch, One Beer" (the original "One Scotch, One Bourbon, One Beer" was by Amos Milburn and His Aladdin Chickenshackers from 1953). Finally, there's Lonnie Johnson's "Fine Booze and Heavy Dues" from 1962. In category 3, there are songs such as Tupac Shakur's 1994 "Pour Out a Little Liquor."

Now we move onto a specific subset of category 2, where specific brands of alcohol (in this case, malt liquor) are extolled to signal power, glamour and wealth—all with the goal of getting you to try it.

RAPPERS NAME-DROPPING MALT LIQUOR BRANDS

In the late 1980s, the guy who ran the Mackenzie River Corporation, who was trying to make his recently released St. Ides Malt Liquor relevant to Blacks, caught wind of some rap lyrics extoling the virtues of Olde English 800, which at the time was the king of malt liquors on the West Coast. He likely heard Eazy-E (Eric Lynn Wright) of N.W.A. in the song "8 Ball" say:

English 800 cause that's my brand
Take in a bottle, 40 quart, or can
Drink it like a madman, yes I do
Fuck the police and a 502
Stepped in the party, I was drunk as hell
Three bitches already said, "Eric yo' breath smell!"
Forty ounces in hand, that's what I got
(Yo man you see Eazy hurling in the parking lot?)

For the uninformed, "502" is police slang for drunk driving. Wanting to take on Olde English 800, the maker of St. Ides in the early 1990s hired a who's who of rappers to create rhymes about St. Ides. Notorious B.I.G. (Christopher Wallace) wrote "The crooked letter, no other beer better." Warren G (Warren Griffen III): "Conjunction junction what's my assumption, I'm sippin' on the St. Ides brew." And finally, Snoop Dogg (Calvin Broadus Jr.):

I'm headin' to the nearest liquor store (What for?)
To get myself some blueberry, you act like you don't know (Oh!)
The new drink provided by St. Ides
Blueberry is my flavor and you wonder why
I'm tellin' all my peoples from the verse off Gin & Juice
'Cause this new taste is guaranteed to get you loose
So dip down, or skip down however you get it
Blueberry is my flavor, let me know if you wit' it.

We conclude with a verse from Ice Cube (O'Shea Jackson):

Gimme that brew, fool, it's a fulltime jack move
St. Ides malt liquor make the black move
And I'd tell any Tom, Dick and Hank
Who bought 8 ball, "You got ganked"
Go with the black, not the copper
'Cause the S-T crooked I is so proper.

When *Boyz n the Hood*, which features Ice Cube and his St. Ides, was released in 1991, the Los Angeles distributor for the brand reportedly could not keep up with the demand for "S-T crooked I."

Of course, not every rapper was on board with the malt liquor gravy train. In Public Enemy's 1991 track titled "1 Million Bottlebags," the intro goes: "Alcohol beverage companies have aimed an inordinate amount of advertising at Blacks; billboards in inner cities, ads in hip-hop magazines, lots of ads on television."

And later, Chuck D (Carlton Douglas Ridenhour) rhymed:

They drink it thinkin' its good
But they don't sell that shit in the white neighborhood
Exposin' the plan, they get mad at me, I understand
They're slaves to the liquor man.

POWER MASTER: THE BRIDGE TOO FAR

At least in one instance, it seems that the federal government somehow gave a damn about what was going on. G. Heilman Brewing Company (yep, the same outfit that outbid Ted Mack for Blatz before he ended up buying Peoples) was getting ready to release a sub-brand of its Colt 45 (yes, the brands moved around a lot), to be called Power Master. Billboard ads for the new malt liquor featured "a black male model and trumped the product's slogan, 'Bold not Harsh,' projecting an image of potency that may appeal to malt liquor's large inner-city market, but which masks an ugly truth" (from a 1991 *New York Times* editorial titled "The Threat of Power Master"). U.S. Surgeon General Antonia Novello got into the act, calling the product's name and marketing campaign "socially irresponsible." The groundswell of protestors made enough of a stink to tank the product launch, and G. Heilman, already in bankruptcy proceedings, lost $2 million. The malt liquor craze reached its zenith around 1996 but started to wane thereafter. Though you can still find it on your local bottle shop's shelves, it has receded back to being a very niche item.

CHAPTER 19

COLONEL ELMER LUCILLE ALLEN

PIONEERING WOMAN CHEMIST

On September 1, 2023, at the Louisville Marriott Downtown, I walked through a booming drumline of local musicians to enter a large conference room. We were there to honor Colonel Elmer Lucille Allen. I had never heard of her, but she had to be a big deal—I mean, the governor of Kentucky had commissioned her a colonel, which is the highest title of honor that can be bestowed in the state. The luncheon was part of the Black Bourbon Society's (BBS) annual convention, Bourbon Boule.

Elmer Lucille Allen. *Samara Davis.*

Born on August 23, 1931, Allen was known as Cile growing up, as both her father and brother shared the first name, Elmer, with her. Her mother, Ophelia, was a maid and cook, and her father worked as a Pullman porter on the L&N train line (just like the murdered Clarence Pullis, who had the misfortune to tussle with Lem Motlow of Jack Daniel's). Allen was the first in her family to graduate from high school. While attending Central High School, she struggled with a stutter. Through hard work, she got the issue under control and went on to deliver her commencement speech without any problems.

She first attended college at Louisville Municipal College, the branch of the University of Louisville established for Blacks. Like all schools in the South at that time, those in Kentucky were segregated, but it wasn't always so. In the early twentieth century, Kentucky's legislature had covered itself in glory by stamping out an integrated college that had operated for years—all because of a dinner at the White House.

INTERLUDE: CARL DAY AND "PREVENTING THE CONTAMINATION OF WHITE CHILDREN IN KENTUCKY"

Kentucky State Representative Carl Day introduced a bill "to prohibit white and colored persons from attending the same school" on January 12, 1904, in the Kentucky House of Representatives. The bill had a very specific target and reason for being brought up. The target was Berea College, which, since 1855, had been the only integrated college in Kentucky—and probably the South, for that matter. And the reason was a recent (October 16, 1901) visit to the White House by one Booker T. Washington for dinner, at the request of President Theodore Roosevelt. Speaking in favor of Day's bill, State Superintendent of Education Harry McChesney had this to say about the interracial dinner: "If the Berea ideas were carried out to logical conclusion, there would be equality of races in Kentucky." Indeed, Day Bill supporters organized a rally outside the Madison County Courthouse in Richmond, Kentucky, where they argued that citizens should support the bill because Berea was teaching African Americans "to be the social equals of the white man and woman." By inviting a Black man to dine at the White House, President Roosvelt didn't freak out only Kentucky lawmakers.

The bill was passed and signed into law by the governor of Kentucky in March 1904 and went into effect in July that year. One curious provision of the new law forbade individual schools from operating separate White and Black branches within twenty-five miles of each other. Perhaps this provision put into effect the author of the law's stated purpose for the bill, as captured in the February 2, 1904 *Courier Journal*: "Mr. Day, of Breathitt, author of the bill, said he had introduced the measure for the purpose of preventing the contamination of the white children of Kentucky."

Berea College was tried, convicted and fined for violating the law, and its appeal was denied when the Kentucky Court of Appeals agreed with the Kentucky General Assembly that the law had a legitimate purpose: to prevent racial violence and interracial marriage. The court of appeals did, however, strike the twenty-five-mile restriction, finding it "unreasonable and oppressive."

In hearing the case in 1908, the U.S. Supreme Court extended the reach of perhaps its worst decision ever. In its opinion in *Berea College v. Kentucky*, the court furthered the ignominious "separate but equal" holding of 1896's *Plessy v. Ferguson* to include colleges and universities chartered by states. The Day Law remained in effect in Kentucky up until it was amended in 1948 and 1950 after being successfully challenged by Lyman T. Johnson, a Central High School teacher who became the first Black student at the University of Kentucky in 1949.

COLONEL ELMER LUCILLE ALLEN CONTINUED

In 1950, the Catholic colleges in Louisville, Nazareth, Ursuline and Bellarmine, Kentucky, began admitting Black students. In 1951, one of those Black students admitted to the all-female Nazareth (now Spalding University) was Elmer Lucille Allen. She graduated with a bachelor of science in general education, with a major in chemistry and a minor in mathematics. After graduating, she worked in a number of jobs both inside and outside the state and ended up at Brown-Forman Distillery as a junior chemist in 1966—the first Black professional at the company. When asked what it was like being the first, she said:

> *Well what it was like was I told them, I was hired to do a job and I was one of three women in the lab and I told them that I was—we was hired to do the same job and that was it—after that, we had no problems. And this white woman, her husband died and I went to the viewing. She was surprised to see me. Well, I work with you, and if I'm a friend of yours, I work with you, and if some member of your family passes, I'm going to go to the funeral or go to the wake. So she appreciated me being there.*

One of her jobs in the lab was to analyze the raw materials that went into a mash bill (corn, rye, barley, etc.). She worked at Brown-Forman for thirty-one years, retiring in the role of senior chemist in 1997. Though a true pioneer in the alcohol industry, she is probably way more famous for her ceramic art. She helped form the Kentucky Coalition of African American Arts and was a founding member of the Arts Council of Louisville.

At that luncheon in 2023, the BBS bestowed on Allen the Bourbon Pioneer Award, and the City of Louisville published a "Distinguished Citizen Proclamation" in her honor. As Samara Davis put it that day, "She made this major contribution to bourbon, but there's still so much to fill, and there's so much to do in order for everything to be really diverse and inclusive in our space." On September 10, 2024, Allen was inducted into the Kentucky Bourbon Hall of Fame, recognized as an individual who had made a significant and transformative impact on bourbon's stature, growth and awareness. It is the highest honor given by the signature industry.

BIBLIOGRAPHY

Alaniz, Maria L., and Chris Wilkes. "Pro-Drinking Messages and Message Environments for Young Adults: The Case of Alcohol Industry Advertising in African American, Latino, and Native American Communities." *Journal of Public Health Policy* 19, no. 4 (1988): 447–72.

American Battle Monuments Commission. "The Harlem Hellfighters: The Most Storied Black Combat Unit of World War I." February 9, 2021. https://www.abmc.gov.

Baumler, Ellen. "Birdie Brown." *Montana Moments* (blog), October 16, 2013. http://ellenbaumler.blogspot.com.

Belleville (IL) News-Democrat. "Barack 'Cîroc' Obama." January 20, 2009.

Berea College v. Kentucky, 211 U.S. 45 (1908).

Blakely, Julia. "Joe Froggers: The Weight of the Past in a Cookie." *Unbound* (blog), Smithsonian Libraries and Archives, November 1, 2016. https://blog.library.si.edu.

Bryant, William Cullen, and Sydney Howard Gay. *Popular History of the United States*. Scribner, Armstrong, 1876.

Burlington (VT) Free Press. "Thirty-Six Stars—Adventures of the Seedy Man—He Tries to Vote." December 3, 1866.

Burnside, Jacqueline. "Day Law." Early History of Black Berea, 2001. https://community.berea.edu.

Center for Women's History and Leadership (Evanston, Illinois). "Truth Telling: Frances Willard and Ida B. Wells—Lynching, the 'Color Line,' and the WCTU Convention 1894." https//scalar.usc.edu.

Center on Alcohol Marketing and Youth (Georgetown University). "Exposure of African-American Youth to Alcohol Advertising." June 19, 2003.

Christman, Kenneth. "Historical Overview of Alcohol in the African American Community." *Journal of Black Studies* 25, no. 3 (January 1995): 318–30.

Cleary, Andrew. "Diageo Turns to Dutch, Diddy Partnership for Vodka Expansion." Bloomberg, October 30, 2009.

Colored American (New York, NY). "The Mixologist Club." November 10, 1900.

Columbia (TN) Herald. "Who Killed Margaret Lear? Some Light on the Astounding Viciousness of the Liquor Traffic in the Southern States, Including our Own Tennessee." June 19, 1908.

Cornish, Samuel, and John B. Russwurm. "The Drunkard's Will." *Freedom's Journal* (New York, NY), July 27, 1827.

Cornish, Samuel, Phillip Alexander Bell and Charles Bennett Ray. *Annual Report of the Temperance Society*. April 29, 1837.

Covington, William. "Stone Cold Marketing: Selling Alcohol to Young African Americans." Black Voices News, November 15, 2012. https://blackvoicenews.com.

Creek County Republican (Sapulpa, OK). "County Jail Cook Shot." December 15, 1911.

Crowe, Charles. "Violence and Social Reform: Origins of the Atlanta Riot of 1906." *Journal of Negro History* 53, no. 3 (July 1968): 234–56.

Crumpton, Taylor. "How Hennessy Found a Home in the Black Community." Zora, August 13, 2020. https://zora.medium.com.

Cunningham, Wesley Sawyer. "Interview with Elmer Lucille Allen." University of Louisville, Black Arts in Louisville, April 4, 2016. https://ohc.library.louisville.edu.

Daily Herald (Biloxi, MS). "Alleged Pirates Operate on Booze Boat Causing Biggest Raid in Years." January 16, 1922.

———. "Must the Coast Carry the Whole Burden?" January 16, 1922.

Daily Mirror (London, England). "Sea Hero Who Saved 110 Lives Honoured." February 26, 1936.

Daily Press (Newport News, VA). "Royal Mint Julep, 1860." November 2, 1951.

Daily Times (Richmond, VA). "John Dabney Dead." June 8, 1900.

———. "The New King's Visit to Richmond." January 23, 1901.

Dent, Bryan. "Last Stop for the Night Train Express." *Modern Drunkard Magazine* 63 (March 2022). https://drunkard.com.

———. "What's the Word? Thunderbird!" *Modern Drunkard Magazine* 59 (2014). https://drunkard.com.

Department of Health and Human Services, Office of the Inspector General. "Youth and Alcohol: Controlling Alcohol Advertising that Appeals to Youth." October 1, 1991.

Dixon, Floyd. "Hey Bartender." Cat Records, 1955.

Dolinar, Brian. "Humor Can Often Make Dents Where Sawed-Off Billard Sticks Can't: The Bootsie Cartoons by Ollie Harrington." *Studies in American Humor* New Series 3, no. 14 (2006): 73–90.

Dougherty, Philip H. "Advertising: Hennessy Sets Broad Appeal." *New York Times*, February 17, 1983.

Douglas, Herbert P. "The HistoryMakers Video Oral History Interview with Herbert Paul Douglas, Jr." February 7, 2005. https://www.thehistorymakers.org/sites/default/files/A2005_039_EAD.pdf.

Douglass, Frederick. *Life and Times of Frederick Douglass*. Collier, 1892.

———. "Temperance and Anti-Slavery: An Address Delivered in Paisley, Scotland on March 30, 1846." In vol. 1 of *The Frederick Douglas Papers: Series One: Speeches, Debates, and Interviews*, edited by John Blassingame et al. Yale University Press, 1979.

Duke, Jane T. "Confederate Veteran Recalls." *Richmond (VA) News Leader*, April 15, 1938.

Durr, Eric. "Hell Fighters Got Heroes' Welcome 100 Years Ago in New York." National Guard, February 4, 2019. http://www.nationalguard.mil.

Ebony. "Hennessy + Blacks, Straight Up." January 18, 2012.

———. "Never Stop, Never Settle: Hennessy Celebrates 250 Years." April 3, 2015.

Edwards, Sherman. "Molasses to Rum." *1776*. Sony Broadway, 1969.

Eisenhart, Dick. "Steuben Winery Auctioned; Owner Says He'll Be Back." *Elmira (NY) Star-Gazette*, July 3, 1974.

Emack, Niko. "Why a Cognac Brand's Marketing Plan Includes a Black Cycling Pioneer." WBUR, August 16, 2019. https://www.wbur.org.

Emen, Jake. "The Cognac Conundrum: Why the World's Most Celebrated Brandy Is Ignored in Its Homeland." VinePair, April 18, 2023. https://vinepair.com.

Encyclopedia.com. "Schieffelin & Somerset Co." https://www.encyclopedia.com.

Eslinger, Ellen. "Antebellum Liquor Reform in Lexington, Virginia: The Story of a Small Southern Town." *Virginia Magazine of History and Biography* 99, no. 2 (April 1991): 163–86.

Evening Bulletin (Charlotte, NC). "Bininger's Old London Dock Gin." December 4, 1860.

Evening Herald (Shenandoah, PA). "Sunshine Brewing Co. Up for Sale." February 4, 1971.

Evening Star (Washington, D.C.). "Colored Men Behind the Bar." March 26, 1903.

Federal Trade Commission. "FTC's Endorsement Guides: What People Are Asking." https://www.ftc.gov.

Fergus County Argus (Lewistown, MT). "Has Fine Still." July 28, 1922.

Fernheimer, Janice W. "90 Years of Elmer Lucille Allen." *American Whiskey Magazine* (November 8, 2021). https://americanwhiskeymag.com.

Fevyer, William H. *Acts of Gallantry Volume Two: Being a Detailed Account of Deeds of Bravery in Saving Life, 1871–1950 for Which the Royal Humane Society Awarded the Silver Medal and the Stanhope Gold Medal.* Naval & Military Press, 1996.

Fields, Jessica. "10 Things You Should Know About Hennessy Cognac." VinePair, https://vinepair.com.

Fulton, Doveanna S. "Sowing Seeds in an Unstilled Field: Temperance and Race, Indeterminacy and Recovery in Frances E. W. Harper's *Sowing and Reaping*," in "Racial Identity, Indeterminacy, and Identification in the Nineteenth Century," *Legacy* 24, no. 2, (2007): 207–24.

GeoGee Experience Magazine. "How Menthol, Malt Liquor, and Black Folks Became Entwined." May 14, 2016. https://medium.com/the-geogee-experience-magazine.

Godsil, Rachel D. "Race Nuisance: The Politics of Law in the Jim Crow Era." *Michigan Law Review* 105, no. 3 (December 2006): 505–57.

Good Life France. "The History of Jazz in Paris." https://thegoodlifefrance.com.

Great Falls Tribune (Helena, MT). "Ten Federal Court Liquor Suits Filed." May 17, 1933.

Guns N' Roses. "Nightrain." *Appetite for Destruction*. Guns N' Roses P&D, 1987.

Halifax (Novia Scotia) Herald. "Julep Cup Preserved." January 26, 1901.

Hans, Nathan. "Dan Emmett and the Rise of Early Negro Minstrelsy." University of Oklahoma Press, 1962.

Hanson, David J. "The Lincoln-Lee Legion: Youths Pledged Alcohol Abstinence." Alcohol Problems and Solutions. https://www.alcoholproblemsandsolutions.org.

Harris, Christopher. "Olympian Herb Douglas Remembers the Legacy He Built in Sports and Business." *Ebony*, March 9, 2017.

Harry, John. "Beer for the People: How Wisconsin's First Black-Owned Brewery Took on the Entire Beer Industry." Good Beer Hunting, July 29, 2020. https://www.goodbeerhunting.com.

Hattiesburg (MS) News. "Nigger Gin Gets Acquittal for Accused." December 17, 1912.

Henderson (NC) Daily Dispatch. "Want to Buy Grapes." September 19, 1940.

Historical Society of the New York Courts. "Trials Relating to the New York Slave Insurrection, 1741." https://history.nycourts.gov.

Hochstein, Morton. "The Legendary Walter Taylor." *Life in the Finger Lakes* (September/October 2017). https://www.lifeinthefingerlakes.com.

Hohwieler, Rupert. "Diageo Enters Cîroc and Lobos 1707 Exchange." Spirits Business, April 7, 2025. https://www.thespiritsbusiness.com.

Horsmanden, Daniel. *The New-York Conspiracy or a History of the Negro Plot.* Southwick & Pelsue, 1810.

Hughes, Langston. *The Collected Works of Langston Hughes: The Early Simple Stories.* Vol 7. Edited by Donna Akiba Sullivan Harper. University of Missouri Press, 2002.

Ice Cube. "Jackin For Malt Liquor." *The St. Ides Bootleg*, 1996.

Idaho Semi-Weekly World (Idaho City, ID). "Powell & Coe." February 5, 1868.

Infante, Dave. "The Sleazy and Spectacular History of Malt Liquor." Thrillist, February 19, 2016. https://www.thrillist.com.

Irwin, Will. "The American Saloon: Ineffective Measures of the Larger Liquor Interests." *Collier's* 41 (May 16, 1908).

———. "Who Killed Margaret Lear?" *Collier's* 41 (May 16, 1908).

Jack Daniel's. "Born to Make Whiskey: The Story of Jack Daniel's." https://jackdaniels.com.

Jack Daniel's Media Site. "Lem Motlow, Jack Daniel's Nephew." https://pressroom.jackdaniels.com.

Jefferson County Tribune (Oskaloosa, KS). "An Inquiry." December 6, 1907.

Jones, Steve. "Bell, One of Spalding's First Black Graduates, Holds Alma Mater Near Her Heart." Spalding University, February 5, 2018. https://spalding.edu.

Kelley, Sean M. "American Rum, African Consumers, and the Transatlantic Slave Trade." *African Economic History* 46, no. 2 (November 2, 2018): 1–29.

Kentucky Historical Society. "Moments in Kentucky Legislative History: Day Law." https://legislature.ky.gov.

Kimbrel, Maggie. "Meet The Makers: Brown-Forman Retired Chemist Elmer Lucille Allen." Bourbon Women, May 10, 2021. https://bourbonwomen.org.

Koren, John. *Economic Aspects of the Liquor Problem*. Houghton Mifflin, 1899.

Lambert, Leigh. "Woburn Plantation Manor House Remains, Burwell Family Cemetery & Nearby Site of Former Woburn Winery." Southern Virginia Homefront, http://sovahomefront.org.

Lanier, Clint. "Yes, Ted Mack Was America's First Black Brewery President." February 12, 2021. https://clintonrlanier.medium.com.

Larkin, J.R. *Alcohol and the Negro: Explosive Issues*. Record Publishing, 1965.

Lee, James F. "Joe Froggers: A Marblehead Taste Tradition." October 4, 2018. https://www.jamesflee.com.

Lewis, Femi. "Diddy Reportedly Made $1 Billion from Diageo Deal Despite Zero Equity in Cîroc Before the Partnership Unraveled." Finurah, January 18, 2024. https://finurah.com.

Lewiston (MT) Democrat-News. "Birdie Brown a Farm Owner Dies of Burns." May 14, 1933.

———. "Birdie Brown Funeral Be 2 P.M. Today." May 15, 1933.

Liberator (Boston, MA). "The Narrative." June 6, 1845.

Litsky, Frank. "Herb Douglas, Olympic Medalist Inspired by Jesse Owens, Dies at 101." *New York Times*, April 24, 2023.

Louisville (KY) Courier-Journal. "Will the Bill Prohibiting the Co-Education of Races Be Reported to the House." February 2, 1904.

Lynch, Doria. US v. Motlow Jack Daniels Conspiracy Remus Presentation. https://www.insd.uscourts.gov.

Madarang, Charisma. "Diddy Accuses Spirits Company Diageo of Racial Discrimination in Lawsuit." *Rolling Stone*, May 31, 2023. https://www.rollingstone.com.

Mandelbaum, David G. "Alcohol and Culture." *Current Anthropology* 6, no. 3 (June 1965): 281–93.

Martin, Ed. "At Woburn Winery, A Labor of Love." *Durham (NC) Morning Herald*, July 30, 1972.

Matthews, Lopez, Jr. "That Cognac Can Get You Into Very, Very Bad Trouble!" *The Text Message* (blog of the Textual Records Division at the National Archives), February 29, 2012. https://text-message.blogs.archives.gov.

McCormack, Lauren. "Joseph & Lucretia Brown." Marblehead Museum. http://marbleheadmuseum.org.

McGuire, John M. "Case History—Poking Around in Old Court Files." *St. Louis Post-Dispatch*, July 31, 1997.

McKinley, J., and S. Maslin Nir. "Sean Combs's White Parties Were Edgy, A-List Affairs. Were They More?" *New York Times*, September 29, 2024.

Midland Journal (Rising Sun, MD). "Some Whiskey Statistics." August 18, 1893.

Mkwesha, Brenda. "Unholy Alliance: How African-American Stars & Big Alcohol Exploit Black People." Movendi, March 1, 2016. https://movendi.ngo.

Montana Record-Herald (Helena, MT). "Four Stills Taken By Federal Agents." May 9, 1933.

Moore, David J., Jerome D. Williams and William J. Qualls. "Target Marketing of Tobacco and Alcohol-Related Products to Ethnic Minority Groups in the United States." *Ethnicity & Disease* 6, Nos. 1–2, Special Double Edition on Racism and Health (Winter/Spring 1996): 83–98.

Morning News (Savannah, GA). "Southern Mint Juleps. Only Old John Dabney Knows How to Make Them." April 3, 1894.

Mosley, Bertha, Bobbie J. Atkins and Michael Klein. "Alcoholism and Blacks." *Journal of Alcohol and Drug Education* 33, no. 2 (Winter 1988): 51–58.

Murthy, T. Virgil. "The Puritan Are Not Your Friends." Addict Collective, April 22, 2023. https://addictcollective.substack.com.

N.W.A. "8 Ball." *N.W.A. and the Posse*, Macola, 1987.

Narvaez, Alfonso A. "William Schieffelin 3d, 67, Dies; Headed Wine and Spirit Importer." *New York Times*, March 24, 1989.

National Archives. "General Correspondence, 1944–1946." National Archives Identifier 5717797. War Department, U.S. Forces, European Theater. Adjutant General Section. Administration Branch. Record Group 498: Records of Headquarters, European Theater of Operations, United States Army (World War II).

Nebraska Signal (Geneva, NE). "Former Nebraskan Honored." June 5, 1919.

Neil, William C. "Death by Whiskey." *North Star* (Rochester, NY), September 29, 1848.

———. "Scientific Darkey Trick." *North Star* (Rochester, NY), September 1, 1848.

New York Age. "First Negro Brewery Launched in Philly." December 3,1955.

———. "Major Arthur Little Commands 15th Reg't." January 8, 1921.

New York Daily Herald. "The Campbells are Coming." March 15, 1854.

———. "Death of Cato of 'The Road.'" February 17, 1858.

New York Times. "Friends of Tuskegee Ready to Celebrate." April 11, 1931.

———. "Fund For Hampton." January 19, 1905.

———. "The Threat of Power Master." July 1, 1991.

New-York Tribune. "Hylan Is Sued by Schieffelin for $100,000." May 3, 1919.

Nobel, L.P. "Defeat of the Liquor Bill." *National Era*, August 21, 1851.

———. "The Law of Slavery in the State of Louisiana (1847)." *National Era*, September 16, 1847.

O'Neil, Tim. "Distiller Beats Murder Charge." *St. Louis Post-Dispatch*, December 8, 2013.

———. "Jack Daniel's Played Prohibition Role." *St. Louis Post-Dispatch*, December 6, 2009.

Onion, Rebecca. "A WWI-Era Memo Asking French Officers to Practice Jim Crow with Black American Troops." Slate, April 27, 2016. https://slate.com.

Oshkosh Beer (blog). "Untangling the History of Ted Mack and Peoples Brewing." March 24, 2019. https://oshkoshbeer.blogspot.com.

Paducah (KY) Sun. "Devil's Island Endurance Gin." March 8, 1905.

———. "A New Enterprise in Paducah." February 15, 1905.

Parr, Christopher. "Diddy and Diageo and Acquire DeLeon Tequila." Pursuitist. https://pursuitist.com.

Partin, Elliot. "Freedom's Journal (1827–1829)" BlackPast, January 4, 2011. https://www.blackpast.org.

Patick, James. "Oak Park Brewing's Newest Is Much More Than a Beer. It's a Black History Lesson." *Sacramento Bee*, August 28, 2020.

Pawnee County (OK) Journal. "Ten Thousand Dollar Stock." November 7, 1907.

Pittsburgh Courier. "Negro Captain Brings First Liquor Cargo Into Port of New Orleans." December 30, 1933.

———. "On the Slightly Intriguing Side…" December 10, 1955.

Plessy v. Ferguson, 163 U.S. 537 (1896).

Prial, Frank J. "For the "First Black Winery in the U.S.' 1973 Was NOT a Good Year." *New York Times*, November 16, 1973

———. "William Jay Schieffelin, Jr., 94 Importer of Wines and Spirits." *New York Times*, May 3, 1985.

Province (Vancouver, British Columbia). "Rap Stars Thirst for Liquor-Brand Status." November 27, 2011.

Public Enemy. "1 Million Bottlebags." *Apocalypse 91…The Enemy Strikes Back*, 1991.

Rainey, Gertrude. "Blues and Booze." *Ma Rainey: Complete Recorded Works in Chronological Order* vol. 2, Document Records, 1997.

REBEAT. "10 Songs from the 1950s About Getting Wasted." https://www.rebeatmag.com.

Rense, Sarah. "I Was the Only Black Man Making Liquor in America. Not Much Has Changed—Except Me." *Esquire*, June 25, 2020.

———. "Jackie Summers Never Gave Up on the Rebirth of Sorel. Fawn Weaver Brought It Back to Life." *Esquire*, October 1, 2021.

Reverly Tours. "The World's Frist Forgotten Celebrity Bartender: Cato Alexander." December 30, 2023. https://revelry.tours/articles/cato-alexander/

Richmond (VA) Times-Dispatch. "Meeting Coming Events." May 5, 1958.

———. "Meetings, Coming Events." September 15, 1949.

Risen, Clay. "Yes, African-Americans Drink Bourbon. You'd Never Know It From the Marketing." *New York Times*, May 20, 2019.

Rorabaugh, W.J. "Alcohol in America," in "Drug Use in History," *OAH Magazine of History* 6, no. 2 (Fall 1991): 17–19.

Rosamie. "A Brief History of Ripple Wine." SloWine, January 10, 2024.

Rucker, Darius. "Beers & Sunshine." *Carolyn's Boy*, Capitol Nashville, 2020.

Russell, Judy. "'Falsehoods' Rapped by Brewery President." *Oshkosh (WI) Northwestern*, April 27, 1970.

Sanders, Tanya, Mark Sanders and William White. "'When I Get Low, I Get High': The Portrayal of Addiction and Recovery in African American Music." *Counselor* 7, no. 6 (2006): 30–35. https://www.williamwhitepapers.com.

Sandford and Son Wiki. "'Ripple' Wine." https://sanfordandson.fandom.com.

Sapulpa (OK) Herald. "Eggs Ain't Eggs; Ella Is Jailed." April 19, 1918.

———. "Green Cloth Knights Caught in Addition." January 30, 1918.

———. "Raid Results in Arrest of Seventeen." February 9, 1918.

Scheufele, Michael. *Jacob Scheuffelin, Currently in Pennsylvania…: Five Hundred Years of the Schieffelin Family.* Wissenschaftliche Buchgesellschaft (WBG), 2022.

Schrad, Mark L. "The Forgotten Black History of Prohibitionism." Politico, February 6, 2021. https://www.politico.com.

Schwarz, Phillip, and Dictionary of Virginia Biography. "John Dabney (ca. 1824–1900)." Encyclopedia Virginia, December 7, 2020. https://encyclopediavirginia.org.

Scott, Emmett J. *Scott's Official History of the American Negro in the World War.* Homewood Press, 1919.

Seattle Post-Intelligencer. "Fine Whiskies." August 13, 1877.

Shaboozey (Collins Chibueze). "A Bar Song (Tipsy). *Where I've Been Isn't Where I'm Going*, Republic Empire, 2024.

Shadd, Mary Ann. "Dr. Hiram Cox, Chemical Inspector of Alcoholic Liquors." *Provincial Freeman*, June 13, 1857.

Snoop Dogg. "Gin and Juice." *Doggystyle*, Death Row Records, 1994.

———. "St. Ides Commercial 2." *The St. Ides Bootleg*, 1996.

Southwestern Elk City (OK) Press. "Gigantic Jewish Liquor Trust And Its Career." January 13, 1922.

Steinberg, Brian. "Diageo Cuts Ties with Sean Combs After Dispute Over Vodka, Tequila Venture." *Variety*, June 27, 2023. https://variety.com.

St. Louis Post-Dispatch. "Final Arguments Made by Counsel in Murder Trial." December 10, 1924.

———. "He Acted to Defend Self." December 11, 1924.

———. "Instructions of Court to Cover Four Verdicts." December 9, 1924.

———. "Motlow Sends Turkey To Each Member of Jury." December 23, 1924.

———. "Motlow Writes of Courtroom Cheering." December 14, 1924.

———. "Testimony for Defense Begins at Motlow Trial." December 5, 1924.

St. Louis Star and Times. "Arguments Given in Motlow's Trial in Pullis Killing." December 10, 1924.

———. "White Witness Agrees." December 5, 1924.

Sullivan, Jack. "Dreyfuss & Weil of Paducah: Gin and Sin." *Those Pre-Pro Whiskey Men!* (blog), March 11, 2013. https://pre-prowhiskeymen.blogspot.com.

———. "How Lem Motlow Got Away with Murder" *Those Pre-Pro Whiskey Men!* (blog), November 26, 2019. https://pre-prowhiskeymen.blogspot.com.

———. "Lee Levy and 'Black Cock Vigor Gin." *Those Pre-Pro Whiskey Men!* (blog), November 29, 2018. https://pre-prowhiskeymen.blogspot.com.

Summers, Jerry. "Lem Motlow: 2 Strikes But Not Out." Chattanoogan.com, October 18, 2020. https://www.chattanoogan.com.

Sun Herald (Biloxi, MS). "Coast Marine Activities Tainted by Blood and Rum." April 23, 1923.

Sykes, Roosevelt. "Devil's Island Gin Blues." 1934. LyricsFreak. https://www.lyricsfreak.com.

Tampa (FL) Times. "British Asked to Seek Maloa." June 15, 1937.

Tampa (FL) Tribune. "Two Hondurans Arrested Here." May 9, 1936.

———. "U.S. Holds Honduran Negro Sailors on Smuggling Charges." May 10, 1936.

Tanzilo, Bobby. "Peoples Was Among America's First Black-Owned Breweries." OnMilwaukee, February 6, 2016. https://onmilwaukee.com.

Times-Democrat (New Orleans, LA). "Evil Brands of Gin Sold In New Orleans." June 29, 1908.

Times Dispatch (Richmond, VA). "Nigger Whiskey." January 14, 1907.

TINA.org. "TINA.org Files Complaint Against Diageo Regarding Its Cîroc Influencers." December 10, 2018; updated January 7, 2019. https://truthinadvertising.org.

2Pac. "Hennessey." *Loyal to the Game*, 2004.

United States v. Motlow, 13 F.2d 645. (M.D. Tenn. 1926).

Walton, Hanes, Jr., and James E. Taylor. "Blacks and the Southern Prohibition Movement." *Phylon* 32, no. 3 (Third quarter, 1971): 247–59.

Washington, Airen. "This Black Women-Led Whiskey Brand Is Honoring the 'Entrepreneurial Spirits' of Female Bootleggers." *Forbes*, August 21, 2020.

Washington Tribune. "James Tells of Russwurm." July 9, 1926.

Weaver, Carly. "Is Vodka Still the Most Valuable Spirit in America?" Daily Meal, February 6, 2023. https://www.thedailymeal.com.

Weaver, Elisha. "Dr. Cox on Beer." *Christian Recorder* (Philadelphia, PA), January 3, 1863.

———. "Whisky and Newspapers." *Christian Recorder* (Philadelphia, PA), December 27, 1862.

Weaver, Fawn. *Love and Whiskey*. Melcher Media, 2024.

Webb, Holland. "Temperance Movements and Prohibition." *International Social Science Review* 74, no. 1/2 (1999): 61–69.

Weekly Arkansas Gazette (Little Rock, AK). "A.M. Bininger & Co." May 26, 1860.

Whiskey University, "Lemuel 'Lem' Oscar Motlow." https://www.whiskeyuniv.com.

White, Josh. "Pigmeat and Whiskey Blues." Document Records, 1935.
Wikipedia. "Day Law." https://en.wikipedia.org.
———. "Andrew Johnson." https://en.wikipedia.org.
———. "*The Christian Recorder*." https://en.wikipedia.org.
———. "Cîroc." https://en.wikipedia.org.
———. "*The Colored American* (New York City)." https://en.wikipedia.org.
———. "Dreyfus Affair." https://en.wikipedia.org.
———. "Elmer Lucille Allen." https://en.wikipedia.org.
———. "Flavored Fortified Wine." https://en.wikipedia.org.
———. "Herb Douglas." https://en.wikipedia.org.
———. "Knights of the Golden Circle." https://en.wikipedia.org.
———. "*The National Era*." https://en.wikipedia.org.
———. "*The North Star* (anti-slavery newspaper)." https://en.wikipedia.org.
———. "*Provincial Freeman* (newspaper)." https://en.wikipedia.org.
———. "William Jay Schieffelin." https://en.wikipedia.org.
Williams, F.B., Jr. "893 Barrels of Jack Daniel's Old No. 7: The Troubles and Trials of Lem Motlow, 1923–1930." *Tennessee Historical Quarterly* 58, no. 1 (Spring 1999): 34–51.
Williams, Nat D. "Down on Beale, Bootsie's a Boost." *Pittsburgh Courier*, February 9, 1952.
Williams, Oscar R., Jr. *Blacks and Colonial Legislation in the Middle Colonies*. Ann Arbor, MI: University Microfilms, 1970. PhD thesis, Ohio State University (microfilm of typescript).
Wine and Spirits Journal. "The Reason Why You Should Celebrate Black History with Cognac." March 7, 2023. https://wineandspiritsjournal.com.
Winkler, Connie. "Money Woes, but No Sour Grapes for Winemaker." *Star-Gazette* (Elmira, NY), December 26, 1973.
Winn, Thomas H. "Race and Politics: Clarksville During the Progressive Period." *Tennessee Historical Quarterly* 49, no. 4 (Winter 1990): 207–17.
Winship, Kihm. "A Story Without Heroes: The Cautionary Tale of Malt Liquor." *All About Beer Magazine* 26, no. 2 (May 1, 2005). https://allaboutbeer.com.
Wolfe, Pedro. "Controversial Watermelon-Flavored Tequila Takes Center Stage in Ongoing Diddy vs. Diageo Lawsuit." Tequila Raiders, July 5, 2023. https://bottleraiders.com.
———. "Sean 'Diddy' Combs Settles Lawsuit Against Diageo, Ends Ownership Stake in Cîroc Vodka, DeLeon Tequila." Tequila Raiders.
Women's History Matters. "Montana's Whiskey Women: Female Bootleggers During Prohibition." Montana Women's History, January 16, 2014. https://montanawomenshistory.org.

Wondrich, David. "The Cunningness Compounders of Beverages: The Hidden History of African-Americans Behind the Bar." Bitter Southerner. https://bittersoutherner.com.

Yacovone, Donald. "The Transformation of the Black Temperance Movement, 1827–1854: An Interpretation." *Journal of the Early Republic* 8, no. 3 (Autumn 1988): 281–97.

INDEX

A

Allen, Elmer Lucille 157–160

B

Beecher, Lyman 69
Bond, Colonel Frank P. 59, 60
Bowie, Robert R. 48
Brown, Bertie "Birdie" 41, 42, 43
Brown, James 19, 29
Brown, Lucretia 148
Burton, Mary 145, 146
Burwell, Armistead 24, 25

C

Cary, Mary Ann Shadd 75
Champale 152, 153
Cîroc 19, 43, 83, 84, 85, 86, 87, 88, 89
Combs, Sean 43, 83, 84, 85, 86, 87, 88, 89
Cox, Hiram 20, 75, 154
Crowe, Dr. Charles 77, 92

D

Davis, Samara B. 17, 133, 134, 135, 160
Day, Carl 158
Dominijanni, Eric 99
Douglas, Herbert Paul 122, 123
Douglass, Frederick 71, 73, 74, 127
Downing, Thomas 46
Dreyfus, Alfred 94
DuBois, W.E.B. 106, 107

E

Edward VII, King 49
Europe, Lieutenant James Reese 113

F

Fedderman, Raymond 21, 23, 24
Ford, Henry 95
Foxx, Redd 30

G

Gallo 28, 29, 30
Garesche, Vital W. 58

H

Harper, Frances Ellen Watkins 79, 80, 81
Henderson, Alan 51
Hughes, Charley 112
Hughes, Langston 136

I

Irwin, Will 89, 90, 91, 92, 93, 95

J

Johnson, Andrew 59, 127, 129, 132
Joseph Schlitz Brewing Company 152, 153

K

Knights of the Golden Circle 130, 131, 132
Koren, John 101, 103, 104, 105, 106, 107, 108

L

Lamb, W.B. 58
Larkins, John R. 38, 142
Lear, Margaret 89, 90, 93
Lincoln, Abraham 120, 127, 131

M

Motlow, Lemuel O. 52, 53, 55, 56, 57, 58, 60, 61, 157

N

Novello, Antonia 156

P

Peay, Austin 57
Pennington, J.W.C. 70
Pullis, Clarence T. 55, 56, 57, 58, 60, 61, 157

R

Reed, Wallace D. 148
Ripple 27, 30
Romero, Cesar 28
Russwurm, John Brown 68

S

Schieffelin, William Jay 112, 118, 119, 120, 122, 123, 124
Semple, Jessie B. 136
Shakur, Tupac 20, 110, 154
Small Business Administration (SBA) 23, 24, 33, 35, 37
Smith, John Randolph 32
Stowe, Harriet Beecher 69
Summers, Jackie 98
Sunshine Brewing 33
Sykes, Roosevelt "Honeydripper" 91

T

Taylor, Walter 22
369th Infantry Regiment 20, 113, 114, 116, 117, 118, 119
Thunderbird 19, 27, 28, 29
Truth in Advertising 85, 86

W

Walker, Hiram 140
Walker, Seth M. 58
Wallis, Ed 55, 58, 60
Washington, Booker T. 78, 118, 120, 158
Webster, Clarence 62, 63, 64, 65, 66
Wells, Ida B. 81
Willard, Frances E. 81
Williams, Evan 50
Williams, William December, Jr. 153

Y

Youle, George 47

ABOUT THE AUTHOR

Isaac F.B. Hughes.

Troy Hughes, compotator extraordinaire, uses his medieval art history degree to its fullest in his side gig producing award-winning bourbons and ryes under the brand Mt. Pleasant Club Whiskey. His day job is as a corporate attorney. On weekends, he sometimes leads a whiskey walking tour of his beloved Washington, D.C. neighborhood Mount Pleasant—except when Arsenal is playing. This is his second book, the first being *Whiskey Makers in Washington, D.C.: A Pre-Prohibition History*. He's a veteran (Aim High!), a cat dad and now a dog dad, and he's very thankful that his wife, Toni, allows him to continue to go down this silly rabbit hole. More on him can be found at https://thecompotator.com, and you can reach him at troy@thecompotator.com.